Evolving Roles of Chief Information Security Officers and Chief Risk Officers

Dr. Michael C Redmond, PhD
(MBA) Retired Major, US Army
MBCP, FBCI, CEM

BookLocker
Trenton, Georgia

Paperback ISBN: 978-1-958891-20-9
Hardcover ISBN: 978-1-958891-21-6
Ebook ISBN: 979-8-88531-607-1

Published by BookLocker.com, Inc., Trenton, Georgia.

BookLocker.com, Inc.
2024

First Edition

Library of Congress Cataloging in Publication Data
Redmond, PhD (MBA) Retired Major, US Army MBCP, FBCI, CEM, Dr. Michael C
Evolving Roles of Chief Information Security Officers and Chief Risk Officers by Dr. Michael C Redmond, PhD (MBA) Retired Major, US Army MBCP, FBCI, CEM
Library of Congress Control Number: 2024916034

Dedication

To my daughter Brie, whom I love unconditionally!

Acknowledgment

Thanks, Baton Mati, for being a great thesis advisor for my thesis on Risk Management

Thanks, Besfort Ahmeti, for being a great thesis advisor for my thesis on Information Security Management

Thanks, Ivana Stevanovic, for your research guidance as the PECB University librarian.

Special Thanks to PECB for partnering with me on the production of this book.

About the Author

Dr. Michael C. Redmond, PhD

Dr. Michael C. Redmond, PhD, has been honored as a Top Woman in her field at a White House Luncheon and was selected out of the world to write the prologue for the chapter on RISK Management by the United Nations for their Disaster Book which was given to the head of state for every UN member nation.

She served for a short time as the US Attaché to Chile for Disaster Recovery at the request of the President of Chile.

Michael is a graduate of Command & General Staff College out of Fort Leavenworth, where she studied strategic planning, control and command, and control in an emergency. Furthermore, she has completed Civil Affairs Advanced courses in the School for Special Warfare, which encompasses planning in various political and cultural environments.

Michael has taught as an Adjunct Professor:

- New York University - Emergency Management and Business Continuity Management
- Master's program at John Jay College- Emergency Management and Business Continuity Management
- St. Thomas School of Law – Masters in Cyber Law
- University of Maryland- Business Management
- Mercy College - Business Management

She is an accomplished professional in the fields of Enterprise Risk Management and Information Security, and she holds two MBA degrees from PECB University, one in Risk Management and the other in Information Security. She has an MBA in International Business and Marketing from Fordham University. She graduated with a Certificate in International Business Operations and Trading from the American Institute of Banking. Michael attended Marymount Manhattan College for a dual major in Communications Arts and Management, with a minor in Secondary Education. Her expertise in these areas has made her a highly sought-after consultant, trainer, auditor, and advisor to large corporations and organizations.

She has served as a remote CISO for organizations and has been serving as the Deputy CISO for Metro Louisville for over two and half years, responsible for Information/Cyber security for 42 agencies, and her expertise in Governance, Risk, and Compliance is a great asset.

Throughout her career, she has demonstrated a deep understanding of the complex challenges facing businesses and has helped numerous organizations develop effective Enterprise Risk Management and Information Security strategies. Michael has been instrumental in the development and implementation of some of the most advanced cybersecurity programs, ensuring companies are protected from cyber threats and data breaches.

She is a highly respected author, educator, and international speaker, well known for her ability to explain complex concepts in clear and concise terms. Michael has authored several notable publications in the field of Business Continuity Management and Information Security, and she is a regular contributor to industry-leading publications and media channels.

One of her most notable achievements is the establishment of Redmond Worldwide, a consulting firm specializing in enterprise risk management and cybersecurity. Under her leadership, the firm has established a reputation as a trusted advisor to leading companies around the world.

Overall, Michael is a highly accomplished professional with a wealth of knowledge and experience in the fields of risk management and information security. Her deep understanding of the challenges businesses face, coupled with her expertise in developing effective strategies, has made her a trusted advisor to organizations of all sizes and industries.

Boards and Associations

CDO Magazine's Global Security Board

Cyber Security Collaboration Forum. Leadership Board

ISC2 NJ Chapter Member

Certifications

Certified as Senior Lead Implementer/Senior Manager:

- ▶ ISO/IEC 27002 Security Techniques Senior Lead Implementer and Auditor
- ▶ ISO/IEC 27005 Information Security Senior Lead Risk Management
- ▶ ISO 31000 Senior Lead Risk Manager
- ▶ ISO 9001 Quality Management Senior Lead Implementer
- ▶ ISO/IEC 27032 Senior Lead Cyber Security Manager
- ▶ ISO/IEC 38500 Senior Lead IT Corporate Governance Manager
- ▶ ISO/IEC 27035 Security Lead Incident Manager
- ▶ ISO/IEC 27001 Information Security Management Senior Lead Implementer
- ▶ ISO 27999 Information Security Management in Health Organizations
- ▶ ISO/IEC 27701 Privacy Information Management Senior Lead Implementer
- ▶ ISO 22301 Business Continuity Management Systems Senior Lead Implementer

- ▶ ISO 55001 Asset Management Senior Lead Implementer
- ▶ ISO 14001 Environmental Management Senior Lead Implementer
- ▶ ISO 26000 Senior Lead Implementer Social Responsibility
- ▶ ISO 37001 Anti Bribery Management Systems Senior Lead Implementer
- ▶ ISO 13485 Medical Devices Quality Management System Senior Lead Implementer
- ▶ ISO 21500 Senior Lead Project Manager

Certified Implementer/Manager – Foundation

- ▶ ISO 22316 Security and Resiliency Management
- ▶ ISO 22320 Emergency Management
- ▶ ISO 20700 Management Consultancy Services
- ▶ GDPR General Data Protection Regulation (EU) 2016/679

Certified as Senior Lead Auditor

- ▶ ISO/IEC 27001 Information Security Management Senior Lead Auditor
- ▶ ISO 22301 Business Continuity Management Systems Senior Lead Auditor
- ▶ ISO 9001 Quality Management Senior Lead Auditor
- ▶ ISO 55001 Asset Management Senior Lead Auditor
- ▶ ISO 14001 Environmental Management Senior Lead Auditor
- ▶ ISO 26000 Social Responsibility Senior Lead Auditor

▶ ISO 37001 Anti Bribery Management Systems Senior Lead Auditor

Other Certifications:

▶ Masters Business Continuity Planning (Disaster Recovery Institute) - MBCP
▶ Masters Business Continuity Planning (Business Continuity Institute) - FBCI
▶ Certified Emergency Manager - CEM
▶ Certified Project Manager – PMP
▶ Certified Trainer PECB
▶ DOD Hazmat
▶ Completed Pandemic Management Training

About Those Thanked

BATON MATI

Director of Academic Affairs, PECB University

As the Director of Academic Affairs, Baton ensures that PECB University continues to live up to its vision as a provider of premium quality study programs, by focusing on the development of new frontiers in the distance-learning platform, overseeing the curricula and the academic staff, as well as supervising the licensing and continual development of study programs at PECB University.

Baton has extensive experience in academia, lecturing both at undergraduate and graduate level courses, as well as being engaged in the continuous improvement of higher education institutions. Furthermore, he is an experienced business consultant as well as a business & economics researcher, having authored various policy papers and managing projects in the domain of education, economic development and entrepreneurship.

Currently a PhD candidate, Baton has received his Master's degrees from Uppsala University as well as ICN Business School in the fields of International Management & Business Studies. He holds a professional Master's degree from the University of Bologna as well.

Besfort Ahmeti

Besfort is a seasoned business professional and accomplished academic. With a wealth of academic experience, he has imparted knowledge in more than five universities. Besfort also holds an MBA and has made valuable contributions to international companies.

His entrepreneurial spirit shines through as the co-founder of two startups and an NGO dedicated to education development. His journey weaves a tapestry of expertise, innovation, and a deep commitment to education.

University of Ljubljana, Faculty of Economics

Doctor of Philosophy (Ph.D.), Marketing Doctor of Philosophy (Ph.D.),

ACT - American College of Thessaloniki ACT

Master of Business Administration (M.B.A.), Marketing

Rochester Institute of Technology

Bachelor of Applied Science (B.A.Sc.), Business Management, Media & Graphic Communications

Ivana Stevanović

Ivana Stevanović is librarian living and working in Kosovo.

Before choosing librarianship as a profession, she was involved in youth activism and politics, investigative journalism, and teaching. Her passion and interest always revolved around two key elements: information and truth seeking, and Ivana kept exploring them through different lenses.

Her journey into the librarianship began 13 years ago, when she started working as the library manager at the American University in Kosovo. Experience from her previous work has naturally blended into unique style and vision for the new role she embarked on.

Ivana holds interest in developing, in the context of the library, learning experiences that are transformative and inspirational. Fusion of information literacy, critical literacy and academic research strategies are her picks for bringing the mentioned experiences to students' awareness. The intersection of learning and cognitive and metacognitive abilities goes under Ivana's personal favorites when it comes to educational impacts.

Some of her past works are in the field of Digital Humanities, Digital Pedagogy, Digital Literacy, Faculty-Librarian collaborative efforts in shaping course curricula, Embedded Librarianship, et al.

Three of her projects have been published as case studies by Association of College & Research Libraries (ACRL) in the compilation: "Faculty-Librarian Collaborations: Integrating the Information Literacy Framework into Disciplinary Courses".

Ivana holds MA degree in Comparative Literature & Serbian Language and Literature, and another MA degree in Media and Communication.

She served as the librarian at PECB University.

Prologue

Dear Reader,

In the current dynamism of technology and threats, the roles of those guarding the data and asset fortress are rapidly transforming. This book is an exploration, a compilation of two thesis projects that dissect the intricacies and forecast the futures of two pivotal positions in any forward-thinking organization—the Chief Information Security Officer (CISO) and the Chief Risk Officer (CRO).

The intention of blending my research on Information Security with my studies on Risk Management within these pages was a conscious and strategic choice. It is meant to offer you, the reader, insight into the CISO's and CRO's evolving roles and their paths over the next five years and beyond.

If you're ready to probe the depths of these roles and their evolution over the next half-decade, engage with me through these pages. Together, we'll explore the contours of change that are shaping the present and future of the CISO and CRO, unraveling their transforming landscape.

Thanks for this opportunity to share my research with you,

Michael

Michael C. Redmond

Table of Contents

The Application and Governance of Cyber Security in Organizations

Michael C. Redmond

A Thesis in the field of Information Security Management

For the degree: Master of Business Administration

PECB University

February, 2023

The Application and Governance of Cyber Security
in Organizations

Author
Michael C. Redmond,
PhD

Supervisor
Besfort Ahmeti, PhD

A Thesis in the field of Information Security
Management

For the degree: Master of Business Administration

PECB University

February, 2023

Abstract

This thesis is a study about the most effective way to utilize Chief Information Security Officers and organize the risk structure within a corporation. The primary goal of Cyber Security in organizations is to strive to achieve the CIA triad of integrity, confidentiality, and availability. The secondary goal is to provide assurance and accountability while being transparent. In addition, other properties, such as authenticity, accountability, non-repudiation, and reliability can also be involved. Cyber Security is a subset of Information security which is the set of processes that maintain the confidentiality, integrity, and availability of business data in its various forms: verbal, written, and electronic. The Sans Institute defines Information security as the processes and methodologies which are designed and implemented to protect the print, electronic, or any other form of confidential, private, and sensitive information or data from unauthorized access, use, misuse, disclosure, destruction, modification, or disruption. (SANS Institute, 2021). In the United States, the (FFIEC) Federal Financial Institutions Examination Council is a formal U.S. government body made up of five banking regulators. It has published a booklet that addresses regulatory expectations. According to the FFIEC, the booklet is "regarding the security of all information systems and information maintained by or on behalf of a financial institution, including a financial institution's own information and that of all of its customers." Cyber Security for the US Banking industry is covered under the FFIEC, and sections of this booklet apply directly to Cyber Security. The American Bankers Association (ABA) website says that banks in the US have the highest level of security. (American Institute of Banking - Banking Topic, 2021) Yet a banking industry=led standard, Sheltered Harbor, is about preparing for the protection of data in such events as a destructive cyberattack. This does not confirm the claim of the highest level of security. Through a combination of qualitative and quantitative methods, this thesis addresses the issue of how cyber security is governed within organizations in the United States and the role of Chief Information Security Officers (CISOs),

Biographical Sketch of the Author

Michael serves as a Deputy Chief Information Security Officer, of a large Metropolitan City. Michael was selected for Women of Distinction Magazine in 2016 for her contribution in Information/Cyber Security field. Michael is in Who's Who among Executives and Professionals and is in the Academic and Professional National Honor Society for Continuity Planners, "Order of the Sword & Shield." She spent 4 years on Active Duty with the United States Army and 18 1/2 years in National Guard and Reserve before retiring as a Lieutenant Colonel. She is a Graduate of Command & General Staff College (Fort Leavenworth), attended Civil Affairs Courses – US Army JFK School of Special Warfare and is Hazmat Trained, DOD Certified. She has been an Adjunct Professor for University of Maryland, Mercy College, New York University, John Jay Graduate School, and St. Thomas University, where she taught Business Management, Cyber/Information Security, Business Continuity, Disaster Recovery, Emergency Management., and Cyber Law. Michael was selected by the United Nations (UN) to write the prologue for the Risk Management Chapter in the UN's book on Disaster Management, which was given to the Heads of States of all member countries and endorsed by Nelson Mandela and President Bill Clinton. She was also invited to attend a luncheon at the White House honoring her and the other attendees as the top women in their respective fields.

Acknowledgements

I would like to extend my gratitude to PECB University for providing a supportive environment to conduct my research.

I am very grateful to Besfort Ahmeti for all the countless hours serving as my Thesis Advisor.

Special thanks to Ivana Stevanovic, PECB University School Librarian, for her guidance in my research.

I wish to pay special regards to my daughter Brie C. Pfisterer for listening and providing objective feedback when I was developing my Thesis Proposal.

It is with great appreciation that I thank the professionals who took part in my focus groups and provided invaluable qualitative data.

Student Declaration

1. I declare that this dissertation is my original work. I further certify that no parts of it, nor its entirety has been previously submitted for a degree, diploma or certificate in any university or other academic/certification body. This dissertation has not been copied from other published materials; be it other students' theses, or based on any other source except those sources that have been cited appropriately throughout this document, or for which there exists an explicit description in the text.

2. I hereby grant permission to PECB University and PECB University Library to lend or copy this dissertation for digital storage, inclusion of the same in the thesis section of the library, and make it available for academic and research purposes.

3. I have read and understood, and also adhere to all stipulations made in PECB University's Academic Dishonesty Policy; as such, I declare that to the best of my knowledge I have not committed any action that can be described as a dishonest practice within the frameworks of this policy.

4. All views and conclusions stated herein represent my views as the author, and they may not necessarily represent the positions or views of PECB University and/or its Faculty.

Dr. Michael C Redmond, PhD

Author   Date & Signature (handwritten)

Michael C. Redmond   _____

Abbreviations

CCISO - Certified Chief Information Security Officer
CISA: Certified Information Systems Auditor
CEO- Chief Executive Officer
CFO- Chief Financial Officer
CDO: - Chief Data Officer
CGEIT : Certified in the Governance of Enterprise IT
CISO- Chief Information Security Officer
CISM- Certified Information Security Manager
CISSP Certified Information Systems Security Professional
CRO - Chief Risk Officer
ERM - Enterprise Risk Management
FFIEC - Federal Financial Institutions Examination Council
GDPA- General Data Protection Act
GSLC: GIAC Security Leadership
HIPAA- Health Insurance Portability and Accountability Act
ISACA- Information Systems Audit and Control Association
ISC2- International Information Systems Security Certification
Consortium
ISSA- Information Systems Security Association
ISO-International Standards Organization (ISO)
NIST- National Institute of Standards and Technology (NIST)
Risk Management Framework.
PCI- Payment Card Industry Security Standards Council
QTE-Boardroom Certified Qualified Technology Expert

List of Tables

List of Figures

Introduction

The research that focuses on the needed background, knowledge and skills of a Chief Information Security Officers (CISO) has witnessed a considerable amount of debate in the recent years. On the other hand, a thorough examination of the underlying issues regarding the changing challenges in the cyber arena lacks proper attention by scholars. Hence, many organizations blame the Cyber Security Officer when there is a successful Cyber-attack, not taking into consideration that the Board of Trustees, and Executive Management were responsible for Governance of the Cyber Programs.

The CISO is responsible for management of the Cyber Security program, including ensuring that staff are trained on security techniques and tools, managing budgets, vendor management, employee management, maintaining metrics and implementing Governance, Risk and Compliance Standards. Even in today's world, the perception of Cyber Risk Management and the proper use of Chief Information Security Officers in organizations is a topic that has not been studied well enough – meaning that the skills needed to perform this function are not clear. Hence, considering the recent events on a global stage that have tested the Chief Information Security Officers role to the limit, this paper re-examined the needed skills of Chief Information Security Officers.

Focus of the Discussion

History has many examples of organizations, or rather the people in the organizations, who have made poor cyber mitigation and response decisions. The impacts of these poor decisions have had different results, but the consequences for some have been devastating. There is enough evidence from the real world to atone for the importance of Chief Information Security Officers and their involvement throughout all organizational activities; such as the selection of vendors, controls to implement, awareness training and so much more. Based on the published research regarding application of Information Security in the Banking Industry, it was witnessed that whereas a lot was debated regarding Information Security in certain areas, the application of regulations lacks proper attention. Hence a number of organizations have been fined for not properly implementing the regulations as intended and for having poor Governance Programs in place. For example, an article in Forbes written by Ron Shevlin stated, "on Aug. 5, the Office of the Comptroller of the Currency (OCC) handed down a cease-and-desist order to Capital One for its "failure to establish effective risk assessment and management processes before migrating its information technology operations to a cloud operating environment." (Nicodemus, 2020)

In October 2020, Citigroup was fined $400 million for a poor governance in the area of Cyber Security. In its consent order the OCC wrote, "for several years, the Bank has failed to implement and maintain an enterprise-wide risk management and compliance risk management program, internal controls, or a data governance program commensurate with the Bank's size, complexity, and risk profile" (Office of the Comptroller of the Currency (OCC), 2020). The Federal Reserve Bank of New York (FRBNY) issued a report in 2020 that includes information pertaining to an educated prediction that if the U.S. five banks that are most active have an attack, it could cause problems with other backs and affect 38% of the network (Harner, Beck, Fisher and Milman, 2020).

In the last four years alone, cyber incidents such as My Heritage, Caribbean Airlines, and Sun Trust are examples where the CISO was challenged. My Heritage breach took place on October 26, 2017 but the company only learned of the Incident on June 4, 2018. A fake website purporting to be Caribbean Airlines, and the attacked hoped to use it as part of a Phishing Attack to gain valuable personal information. Caribbean Airlines urged its' customers to be aware of impersonators. Sun Trust offered identity protection to all of its clients free of charge when a possible insider threat was found. It was believed that a former employee may have attempted to download information on 1.5 million clients and share it with a criminal third party. The employee was not authorized to access that level of information and the company reviewed its systems and capabilities. Since these events took place there have been countless successful cyber-attacks such as Equifax, CISCO, Colonial Pipeline, and Drop Box. These attacks gained much publicity. The countless companies who did not have an attacks either because of sheer luck of not being attacked, or because of the work of a great Cyber Information Security Officer.

Problem Definition

When a Cyber Incident occurs the Chief Information Security Officer is often the "scape goat" and replaced. In this sense, this thesis seeks to identify what the roles of Executive Management, Board of Trustees and Board of Directors should be in mitigating risks associated with possible cyber threats. Also, what background and skill sets should a Chief Information Security Officer possess.

Study objectives and relevance

The defined problem is that companies experience events that they later reflect, in hindsight, could have been mitigated if they had recognized the risks. This thesis seeks to tackle this issue by conducting a compressive literature review and cross referencing the findings with representatives of the field currently in office. The main study objective is to see whether the scholar and professional interpretations and definition of Cyber Information Security Officers roles and skillsets agree.

All this is relevant because it will enable a better way to hire and utilize Cyber Information Security Officers in the organization. It will also be a guide for Cyber Information Security Officers to ensure their skills are current based on the changing requirements for CISO's.

Literature Review

History of Chief Information Security Officer

The emergence of the Chief Information Security Officer (CISO) executive title in 1995 marked a significant step forward for businesses when it came to protecting the security of their internal technology infrastructures. The Institute of World Politics recognized this growing need and developed the CISO role to address it (Institute of World Politics, 2020). Steve Katz is an influential figure in the world of information security, having made history by becoming the first Chief Information Security Officer (CISO) ever. His dedication to security concepts began in the 1970s and his career soon progressed to leading a security department in the 1980s. However, it was only in the mid-1990s that he became a CISO (Townsend, 2021).

In 1995, Michael Katz joined Citicorp/Citigroup in the wake of a Russian cyber-attack. His appointment marked a major milestone for the industry, as he was the first ever Chief Information Security Officer to be appointed. During his tenure at Citi, Katz was instrumental in promoting greater security measures and protocols to ensure the safety and instituted a security program that was companywide (Katz, 2019). With the dawn of the 21st century, the role of Chief Information Security Officer (CISO) had evolved to incorporate management responsibilities for e-business collaborations and data exchanges across multiple institutions. This was then followed by a significant economic downturn in 2001, causing a subsequent requirement to re-align and reinforce CISO roles to ensure appropriate financial justification.

As Doyle wrote in an article, "by the year 2000, CISO responsibilities included management of e-business alliances and cross-institutional data exchanges. After the economic downturn of 2001, the role began to shift once again. After a few more responsibility reshuffles and higher investment justification due to the potential disruption from threat actors, the role started to feel steadier. In recent years, the role has progressed from a technically oriented, stereotypically geeky, lower-level position, to one that requires a new command of the space that it occupies… at the executive-level." (Doyle, 2022).

Increased Need for Information Security Risk Management

The complexity and interconnectivity of modern digital infrastructures has heightened the need for robust security. In recent years, threat actors have become increasingly sophisticated and capable of perpetrating advanced cyberattacks, with nation states, criminal organizations, and terrorist groups at the forefront. These malicious actors are motivated by a variety of factors including financial gain. Brooks wrote, "the new reality is that almost all critical infrastructures operate in a digital environment, and while the information technology landscape has greatly evolved, so have the vulnerabilities." (Brooks, 2020) With the prevalence of digital technologies and the ever-increasing use of online services, cyber-attacks have become a much deeper concern for businesses across many industries.

However, this danger is especially concerning for financial firms; reports indicate that they are attacked up to 300 times more often than other companies in any given year (Muncaster, 2015). In 2013, one of the most talked-about cyber security incidents occurred at retail chain Target Stores, where hackers were able to gain access to their internal network. The initial point of entry for the hackers was a control system on the store's air conditioning units which had been connected to the internet (Kaplan et al., 2020). The upsides for social and economic development are enormous: the Internet brings global reach to growing numbers of previously isolated individuals and communities. However, a proven and prudent approach such as ISMS is needed to mitigate the downsides. (Lewis, 2019)

Establishing Information Security in Organizations

A security policy is an important and necessary element of any organization, as it provides a framework for managing access to the company's systems and the information contained within them. A well-crafted security policy not only safeguards assets, resources and data, but also acts as a statement both employees and to external entities regarding the organization's commitment to security (NCES, 2023).

Chief Information Security Officer (CISO) Training

Organizations must be particularly mindful of their cyber-security practices, as attacks are now a pervasive concern that cannot be overlooked. While organizations may never achieve total immunity from these malicious assaults, they can take measures to minimize any harm caused when an attack does transpire. An efficient way to facilitate this is via the enforcement of a comprehensive information security management program (O'Flaherty, 2022). Many employers in the field of cybersecurity require applicants to have not just a relevant degree, but also 10 years of experience in related security fields and leadership. Degrees such as information assurance, computer engineering, and computer forensics are all considered highly valuable when applying for positions dealing with cybersecurity (Wintemute, 2022).

There is no one certification that is required for all Chief Information Security Officers (CISO) to obtain; however, there are a number of certifications that can be helpful in demonstrating the knowledge and experience required for successful leadership in the cybersecurity field.

Examples of relevant cybersecurity certifications include:

- ISO/IEC 27001 Information Security Management System
- ISO/IEC 27002 Information Security Controls
- ISO/IEC 27005 Information Security Risk Management

- ISO/IEC 27032 Lead Cybersecurity Manager
- ISO/IEC 27035 Incident Management
- ISO/IEC 27701 Security Techniques for Privacy Information Management
- Lead Cloud Security Manager (Covers ISO/IEC 27017 and ISO/IEC 27018)
- CISSP: Certified Information Systems Security Professional
- CCISO: Certified Chief Information Security Officer
- CGEIT : Certified in the Governance of Enterprise IT
- CISM: Certified Information Security Manager
- CISA: Certified Information Systems Auditor
- GSLC: GIAC Security Leadership

CISO in the Organizational Structure

Where the role of Chief Information Security Officer (CISO) is placed in the organizational chart is rapidly changing and evolving. In some cases, the CISO is under the direct supervision of the Chief Information Officer (CIO), in other companies they report to the Chief Executive Officer (CEO), and surprisingly, in a few instances, the challenge has been -- and continues to be -- that to manage information security risks well requires a specialized set of skills, but this must be balanced against the need to reduce internal conflict of interest when allocating resources and having objectivity within the business in addressing these risks (Kovsky, 2019). According to Pritchard. the idea of an "office of the CISO", or a multiple CISO structure, has been gaining traction in recent years. This type of organizational model typically involves appointing a "super CISO" who is responsible for overseeing overall security and risk management for an organization. The super CISO would then delegate responsibilities tother version could see security leaders aligned by function, with a CISO for manufacturing, for the supply chain, and for the CTO's office, as some examples (Pritchard, 2021).

The role of the Chief Information Security Officer (CISO) is becoming ever more critical in today's highly interconnected digital landscape. As cyberattacks become increasingly prevalent and diverse in nature, organizations need to take a holistic approach to security—one that involves both physical and digital protection strategies, in addition to implementing technical solutions. They must also be very competent in Governance, Risk and Compliance and be able to speak with the business units.

In search for the Perfect Job Description of a CISO

While conducting my secondary research, the same theme kept appearing in many of the recent documents reference a CISO's changing job description. As technology continues to evolve and become more sophisticated, it is increasingly important for the job description of a Chief Information Security Officer (CISO) to be updated regularly. A CISO is responsible for developing, implementing and maintaining the security policies of an organization, so it is essential that their job role encompasses all the latest threats and trends in cybersecurity. By updating the CISO job description regularly with new skills and knowledge, organizations ensure they have a security professional who can provide insights into advanced solutions while also staying ahead potential threats.

As technology continues to evolve and become more sophisticated, it is increasingly important for the job description of a Chief Information Security Officer (CISO) to be updated regularly. A CISO is responsible for developing, implementing and maintaining the security policies of an organization, so it is essential that their job role encompasses all the latest threats and trends in cybersecurity. By updating the CISO job description regularly with new skills and knowledge, organizations ensure they have a security professional who can provide insights into advanced solutions while also staying ahead potential threats. In order to protect an organization's data, operations, and assets, it is essential to hire a Chief Information Security Officer (CISO) that has a strong background in Governance Risk and Compliance (GRC). A CISO with GRC knowledge will be able to create preventative measures that protect the company from threats like data breaches and malicious attacks. Additionally, they will have the experience necessary to develop policies and procedures that ensure the organization meets regulatory requirements. A CISO with GRC expertise will also be able to manage security efforts more effectively due to their deep understanding of an organization's needs.

A Chief Information Security Officer (CISO) is the process owner of all assurance activities related to maintaining the availability, integrity and confidentiality of customer, business partner, employee and business information. The CISO works with executive management to define acceptable levels of risk for the organization while also developing and executing a corporate-wide information security management program that protects the organizations assets (TalentLyft, 2023). A Chief Information Security Officer (CISO) is a senior executive responsible for protecting the organization's information and systems from unauthorized access, damage or misuse. They play an important role in developing and managing security policies and programs, ensuring compliance with applicable laws and regulations, educating staff on security risks, monitoring networks for security breaches, responding to cyber threats. (Cyber Security Jobs, 2023)

Modern CISO

This senior C-level job role involves the implementation of security systems and procedures that will ensure the robustness and safety of its infrastructure, IT projects, and other associated systems. It is the CISO's responsibility to oversee and manage all teams. As stated by Holmes, "where a traditional CISO was a technical influencer, a modern CISO serves as a business influencer who translates cyber risk to business risk .A CISO is a problem solver, a leader, and a strategic thinker. Today, they shape and influence risk decisions to enhance cybersecurity posture. They are heavily involved in building out a full information security program, ensuring that: sensitive data and information stays secure; data is always accurate, hardware and software systems are maintained properly." (Holmes, 2022)

Governance, Risk and Compliance Related to Information Security

According to FFIEC IT Examination Handbook, the board of directors, or a designated board committee, should be responsible for overseeing the development, implementation and ongoing maintenance of the information security program of an organization, as well as holding senior management accountable for its actions. The board should have a thorough understanding of both the business case for information security and the implications that information security risks can have on the organization. The Handbook states that the board of directors should "provide management with direction; approve information security plans, policies, and programs; review assessments of the information security program's effectiveness; and, when appropriate, discuss management's recommendations for corrective action.

The board should provide management with its expectations and requirements and hold management accountable for central oversight and coordination, assignment of responsibility, and effectiveness of the information security program." (FFIEC, 2016). ISO/IEC 27001 is an internationally recognized standard for the implementation of effective security management systems (ISMS) that provide organizations with the necessary guidance and controls to protect their sensitive data and resources. The ISO/IEC 27000 family consists of more than a dozen standards that serve as a comprehensive set of best practices for protecting against potential threats (ISO, 2022).

Data Governance

Data has become an integral part of the modern digital economy, and organizations are leveraging the power of data to improve their financial outcomes and enhance patient care, consumer engagement, and market expansion. Therefore, a well-structured data governance plan has become a necessity for these organizations, which is why they have started empowering their Chief Data Officers (CDO). CISOs play a significant role in data governance initiatives as they are in charge of controlling and securing organizational data. The lifecycle of data governance starts with the generation of important information, followed by collection, processing, storage and eventually destruction when no longer needed. It is therefore essential for CISOs to be aware of all steps in data governance and security (Hughes, 2022).

Risk Management

The job of a Chief Information Security Officer (CISO) has become increasingly important in today's ever-evolving digital landscape, which is facing an onslaught of sophisticated cyberattacks. As the number and severity of these threats continue to grow, CISOs must ensure that their organization's networks and data remain secure—but also the very also the reputation of their organizations. Correia wrote, "CISOs are getting much more deeply involved in organizations – beyond simple technology security matters. That includes an increasing focus on risk management, not just from a threat perspective –

but also from an operational and business logic perspective." (Correia, 2022).

The changing threat landscape in the digital world has made the role of Chief Information Security Officer (CISO) one of the most important roles in any C-level executive team. As cyberattacks become more and more sophisticated, CISOs are faced with the responsibility of protecting not only corporate networks and data, but also the very integrity of their organizations. Business Continuity and business security have long been seen as two separate processes, each with their own distinct methods and approaches. However, the changing nature of cyber threats has meant that companies must now take a more holistic perspective when it comes to ensuring the safety and protection of their assets. As such, merging cybersecurity with Business Continuity and Disaster Recovery (Bowen, 2022).

Business Continuity Management (BCM) is an essential component for achieving cyberattack resilience. It focuses on preparing organizations for various disruptive incidents, such as natural disasters, data breaches, infrastructure failures, and more. BCM activities involve developing plans to ensure that the organization can remain operational during and after a disruption (Kuppinger, 2019). In order to ensure the most comprehensive risk management initiatives, CISO's must have an intimate understanding of how business continuity processes and information security measures are intertwined. Information security can play a crucial role in helping to identify potential threats and risks that could adversely impact the continuity of a business, while effective implementation of business continuity strategies such as disaster.

Compliance

Complying with privacy and security laws is vastly more complex than many assume; it is not only an IT matter but also involves developing, implementing, and enforcing appropriate policies, procedures, and education. In order to ensure that all of their regulatory obligations are met and compliance is maintained, successful CISOs must take a comprehensive approach (Redmon, 2017). CISOs face a considerable challenge when attempting to adhere to multiple frameworks and regulations in the current digital landscape. Companies that operate on an international scale must not only comply with local privacy and data protection laws, but also with global regulations, making the process of management rather complex. This issue is further exacerbated by the fact that data protection regulations are becoming more exacting and with increased requirements. (Gorge, 2022)

Threats and Risks Change Over Time

AI, automated botnets, Internet of Things (IoT), and cloud computing have drastically changed the cyber risk landscape by facilitating attacks with a quicker speed and greater sophistication that was previously unseen. Malicious actors are now able to deploy automated phishing tools, crypto mining software, and other nefarious technology at scale and with ease to launch cyber-attacks (Deloitte, 2019).

Conclusion of Literature Review

The Chief Information Security Officer (CISO) is an executive title that originated in 1995 to address the need for businesses to protect their internal technology infrastructures. The prevalence of digital infrastructures has led to a greater need for robust security, as threat actors continue to develop more sophisticated methods of attack. Nation states, criminal organizations, and terrorist groups all have various motives including financial gain behind their malicious activities. According to Brooks, "the new reality is that almost all critical infrastructure systems are vulnerable to attack." As such, it is essential to take steps to ensure the security and resilience of digital infrastructures.

The board of directors or a designated committee should be responsible for overseeing the development and maintenance of the organization's information security program, while holding senior management accountable. They must understand the business case for information security as well as the implications that information security risks can have on the organization. Organizations must be aware of the looming threat of cyber-attacks and take measures to minimize harm if one were to occur. A comprehensive information security management program is a highly effective way to ensure that organizations are properly protected against these malicious assaults.

In the current business climate, the role of Chief Information Security Officer (CISO) is rapidly evolving and its placement in the organizational chart is changing. The CISO may be under the direct supervision of either the Chief Information Officer (CIO) or the Chief Executive Officer (CEO). Moreover, a specialized set of skills are necessary to successfully manage information security risks. This continues to be a challenge for most companies. The role of the Chief Information Security Officer (CISO) is becoming increasingly important as cyberattacks become more frequent and diverse. Organizations must take a comprehensive approach to security that involves physical, digital, and technical solutions as well as strong governance, risk, and compliance knowledge. They must also be able to communicate effectively with the business to ensure their strategies are aligned.

The Chief Information Security Officer (CISO) is responsible for managing the organization's information security program, ensuring the availability and integrity of all customers, business partner, employee and business information. The CISO works with executive management to develop policies and procedures that protect organizational assets from risks while maintaining acceptable levels of risk throughout the organization. A CISO's role has transformed from traditionally being a technical influencer to now being a business influencer, acting as the bridge between cyber risk and business risk. They are problem-solvers, leaders, and strategic thinkers; their focus is on developing and influencing risk decisions for improving cybersecurity posture. They are responsible for Information and Cyber security Governance, Risk and Compliance To ensure that important data and information remains secure, these protectors of digital assets must also make sure that records are accurate and that hardware/software systems are up-to-date.

With the increase of cyberattacks and digital threats, the role of Chief Information Security Officer (CISO) has become one of utmost importance in C-level executive teams. CISOs are responsible for not only keeping corporate networks and data safe, but also safeguarding the integrity of the entire organization. In addition, Business Continuity and Business Security have been traditionally seen as two distinct processes, yet today both are essential for a successful enterprise strategy and the CISO should have a good working knowledge. CISOs face a major challenge in terms of keeping up with the numerous frameworks and regulations imposed by both local and global laws in the digital age. This is made more difficult due to the ever-increasing complexity and exacting nature of data protection measures.

AI, automated botnets, IoT, and cloud computing have significantly disrupted the cybersecurity landscape by making it easy to launch cyber-attacks with a quicker speed and greater sophistication than ever before. Malicious actors can now deploy automated phishing tools, crypto mining software, and other malicious technologies at scale with ease.

Organizations, boards, and executives are increasingly recognizing the importance of governing risks and establishing guidelines based on ethics, morals, and good business practices. As the business environment continues to evolve, these same organizations must adjust their approach in order to handle any changes or risks that may arise. To ensure success, organizations need to stay up to date with standards and regulations.

Research Questions

Following the extensive literature review, it became obvious that there is a general confusion when it comes to defining the roles of Chief Information Security Officers across industries. The role of Chief Information Security Officers is changing as risks change and CISO's are continually taking courses and learning new skills. The question is which courses and skills do they need and will need over the next five years. Not all organizations have a clear understanding of the role, and are either underutilizing the CISO, having them serve in the role of a technologist which could be better served by a Security Analyst, or not using them effectively in Governance, Risk and Compliance areas. The main question that arises is to whom they should report in the organization to be most effective.

This thesis resulted in the following research questions that would lead to a better understanding of mitigating risk and integrating corporate risk management:

- How is Cyber Security governed within organizations within the United States?
  - *Who is responsible for the governance, risk and compliance of Information and Cyber Security withing the organization?*
- What role do the Boards of Directors actually play in the Governance of Cyber Security?
- What role does the Chief Information Security Officer have in Cyber Security Governance?

- o *What skills and certifications should CISO's acquire to be most effective?*
- o *What should a CISO be responsible for? What is a true definition of a CISO?*
- o *To whom should the CISO report to?*

Answering these questions would help in understanding if Chief Information Security Officers are being used properly or what skills should they process now and over the next five years.

Research Methodology

Research Strategy and Research Process

Planning for the research strategy for this paper is highly related to cross-referencing the already established connotations of the current extent of Chief Information Security Officers responsibilities, with the actual (and changing) practices of the CISO profession in real life. The research approach included researching the premise and various scenarios that may provide different interpretation or insight over the defined problem. Initially, information was gathered from periodicals and rent publications from the past five years. Specifically, due to the nature of the research question, when it comes to the primary research, a qualitative approach fitted the thesis naturally, especially using Focus Groups as a targeted population sample.

The main goal of the research process is to provide objective quantitative and qualitative insights about the scope of the Cyber Security in organizations, which would result in a relatively agreed upon definition – as a result of merging theory and practice on this topic. To get the objective results from a quantitative study, the research was conducted in two sets of open-end question surveys using the Delphi Method. The Delphi Method "is a process framework based on the results of multiple rounds of questionnaires sent to a panel of experts." (Twin, 2020) This entailed different rounds of questionnaires being sent to a focus group of experts made up of Information/Cyber Security Officers who have over 10 years' experience in the field. The focus group members were from the United States, I based the sampling on the research.

A questionnaire survey was developed and distributed to the focus group via email. The responses were then compiled and analyzed. The research strategy was to analyze using a qualitative approach. The results were then shared with the focus group panel of experts after the first questionnaire survey set was conducted by including them in the next questionnaire survey. The results were then culled down even further for commonality by including them in the creation of the next questionnaire survey which was given to the same focus group. The responses were again analyzed systematically in the same fashion to the first time, and the final results for the focus group were determined.

To add another perspective to the research problem, a separate questionnaire survey was conducted which was comprised of questions based on the final results of the focus group questionnaire survey. This survey's population was diverse and targeted – the respondents were top tier managers and auditors who as employees, interact with the Risk Manager as part of their role. Ninety anonymous participants for the second questionnaire were sourced from Information/Cyber Security Managers. These respondents came from LinkedIn, ISC2, the Cyber Security Collaboration Forum, and CDO Magazine's Syber Security Conference speakers.

Nature of Data

Data collected was qualitative and quantitative. The data was derived from both primary and secondary sources. I utilized secondary sources including existing research and studies, articles, periodicals, books, and journals by using data generated from desktop research. All the primary data research was conducted expressly for the purposes of this thesis.

Data Reliability and Relevance

In order to ensure that the focus-group data is as reliable as possible, I repeated the survey twice using the Delphi method, and in two different formants both open-end answer & multiple choice in order to check whether there were answer variations from the participants for the same questions. The reliability of the secondary data is based on the peer-published articles found through academic databases such as ProQuest, as well as publishing houses that cover books etc.

Whereas considerable effort has gone into this research, especially towards impartiality and objectivity, there is always the case that having a larger sample size may add value to this research and provide further arguments to the changing concepts of the roles of Chief Information Security Officers in today's world. This research and the data that I have used and generated is relevant for the academia and the risk management profession. It shows only the development in Risk Management but also where weaknesses in the use of Risk Managers still exists in some organizations and how they can be used more effectively.

A qualitative analysis was done using two focus groups since it is impossible to survey the entire population because of cost, time and practicality. One focus group of Risk Managers for the first part of the research, and a more diverse group of top tier managers and auditors for the second part of the research. There is limited research in this field and many of the articles and periodicals were written prior to the last ten years. The last decade has experienced many international and technological changes that affect business risk that affect Risk Managers and there has been little coverage of the effect.

This thesis is based on the opinions of many professional from diverse organizations. The research showed that the role of the CISO has changed over the last five years, and is anticipated to change more over the next five years. The CISO is no longer a technician but a member of the C (Corporate) level management, responsible for Information Security Governance, Risk and Compliance while also managing the Cyber Analysts and Security Operations Center. They are responsible for protecting the organizations assets from cyber-attacks and ensuring the confidentiality, integrity, and availability of data.

Data Analysis

The analysis was conducted utilizing qualitative and quantitative methods. I conducted the focus-group survey twice in succession using the Delphi Method using a group comprised of international risk managers from a varied group of industries. I chose the Delphi Method because of the accuracy of the results collected from structured groups as opposed to unstructured groups. The initial Focus Group 'interview sheet' included open end questions and answers. All of the focus group participants gave their own opinion without being bound/biased by multiple choices or knowing the other focus group members' opinions. By utilizing open end questions, I was able to elicit relevant information without limiting their answers. In the second round with the Focus Group, I aggregated their replies in 3 multiple choice questions and asked them to find a majority opinion. The questions were prepared by extrapolating the resulting answers that the majority of respondents agreed upon in the initial Focus Group 'interview sheet' and incorporating them into the multiple-choice questions. To recapitalize, after the first round, the answers were analyzed and grouped by similarity into a summarizing response – which were then written down as multiple-choice options for the same questions asked in the initial survey

The first time I sent the Focus Group questionnaire survey 'interview sheet' with open ended answers, where all focus group participants gave their own opinion without being bound/biased by multiple choices or knowing other focus group members' opinions. After the first round the answers were analyzed and grouped by similarity into a summarizing response – which were then written down as multiple-choice options for the same questions that were asked in the initial survey. These were resent as a second Focus Group survey to the same participants to have them review the answers and either confirm or change their response from the first survey after rereading the response. This enabled the convergence to the answer that most closely represented the weighted opinions of all focus group participants.

For the second part of the research, I then targeted top tier business managers and auditors who are employees of organizations from around the world with a survey based on the results of the focus group survey. This led to a better benchmarking of the focus-group survey findings who shared the inside perspective of Information/Cyber Security Managers, with other managers in organizations who shared their opinion as non-professionals in the field.

Research Analysis

The analysis was conducted utilizing qualitative and qualitative methods. I conducted the focus-group survey twice, in succession, using the Delphi Method - using a group comprised of US CISO's from a varied group of industries. I chose the Delphi Method because of the accuracy of the results collected from structured groups as opposed to unstructured groups.

The initial Focus Group 'interview sheet' included open-ended questions and answers. All of the focus group participants gave their own opinion without being bound/biased by multiple choices or knowing the other focus group members' opinions. By utilizing open-ended questions, I was able to elicit relevant information without limiting their answers.

In the second round of the Focus Group, I aggregated their replies into choice questions and asked them to find a majority opinion. The questions were prepared by extrapolating the resulting answers that the majority of respondents agreed upon in the initial Focus Group 'interview sheet' and incorporating them into multiple-choice questions. To recapitalize, after the first round, the answers were analyzed and grouped by similarity into a summarizing response – which were then written down as multiple-choice options for the same questions asked in the initial survey. This enabled the convergence to the answer that most closely represented the weighted opinions of all focus group participants.

For the second part of the research, I then targeted CISO's and Senior Cyber Security Personnel who are employees of organizations from the United States with a survey based on the results of the focus group survey. This led to a better benchmarking of the focus-group survey findings who shared the inside perspective of Information/Cyber Security Managers, with other managers in organizations who shared their opinion as Cyber Security professionals in the field.

Research Results

This research will provide organizations with the necessary tools to ensure that their Chief Information Security Officers are optimally trained to handle their evolving roles, as well as guidance on what additional skill sets may be necessary.

The Chief Information Security Officer (CISO) is responsible for establishing the enterprise's security strategy and roadmap. They collaborate with various departments such as Engineering, Product, IT, and Compliance to ensure that their strategic goals are met in terms of application security, corporate security, and data governance. Additionally, they create, implement, and maintain a security team along with policies, procedures, standards, and guidelines to work with customers. Below, I present the results of this study.

Part 1: The Focus Groups

The first questionnaire survey distributed to the focus group was the open-end answer survey. These results were compiled by similarities in responses to create the second survey where the seven focus group members selected the response for each question that they most agreed with. Below are presented the results from the first focus group, which was the foundation for the second focus group, and the results from the second focus group.

Table 1. Results from Focus Groups - Question

Q	What is a common definition for a Chief Information Security Officer (CISO) in an organization?
	Responses: A 3; B 1; C 1; D 2
A	Responsible for defining its strategic goals as they pertain to application security, corporate security, and data governance. The CISO sets the vision for its enterprise security strategy with a clear roadmap and work closely with its leadership team across Engineering, Product, IT, and Compliance to make sure the roadmap is executed. They create, implement and maintain a security team, build on existing security policies, procedures, standards, and guidelines, and work with customers and prospects to address security concerns. Responsible for developing and implementing an information security program which entails day to day operations, which includes strategy development, operations of information and cyber security operations, budget, and project management and staffing.
B	The Chief Information Security Officer (CISO) is the head of IT security, driving the IT security strategy and implementation forward while protecting the business from security threats and cyber-hacking. The Chief Information Security Officer is responsible for providing strategic thought leadership and measurable, defined outcomes in the oversight and delivery of a robust enterprise information security program. Key focus areas are in the establishment and direction of developing,

	implementing, sustaining, and enhancing enterprise information security and risk management programs Design and oversee the security related projects, as well as projects that require a security component. Keep management informed on the progress that has been made. Ensure that adequate governance is performed through the data lifecycle of firm data. Ensure that regulations are being met, keep employees and management current of the latest news that could impact the security of the firm and audit our security policies that we have developed and enacted to mitigate our security risks
C	A CISO is the role performed by a senior-level executive within an organization responsible for establishing and maintaining the infosec roadmap to protect the employees, customers and shareholders from harm. This role is sometimes fulfilled by a dual-titled CIO/CISO or CSO/CISO depending on the size and maturity of the organization. A business leader charged to build, manage, and maintain the company's security program. Responsible for implementing technical security controls and reducing cyber risk. Accountable to the Board of Directors, and charged with protecting the organization's digital assets and data, aligning security programs with business objectives, managing security, and reducing risk

| D | CISO is responsible for ensuring the confidentiality, integrity and availability of an organization's information, whether it is in digital and physical format and regardless of where it is stored. A senior-level executive responsible for developing and implementing an information security program, which includes procedures and policies designed to protect enterprise communications, systems and assets from both internal and external threats. Develop enterprise-wide security programs to protect corporate systems as well such as the cloud platform for delivering security rating services to customers, executives and the boards of directors |

When asked "What is a common definition for a Chief Information Security Officer (CISO) in an organization?", in the first focus group, four main definitions/descriptions were identified (see Table 1). In the second focus group, most participants agreed that the third and fourth option are better definitions of a CISO.

Table 2. Results from Focus Groups - Question 2.1

Q	Which of these knowledge areas/experiences are critical for a Chief Information Security Officer (CISO)? Governance, Risk and Compliance
	Responses: A 4; B 1; C 2; D 0
A	CISO drives policies and procedures to manage compliance to controls, measurement of key performance indicators, and management decisions against the data to ensure organization goals are being met. The CISO needs

	to assess the risks that could impact the goals of the organization, and plan, test and have contingencies for continuous operations. Compliance to the controls is supported through aligned evidence and reporting.
B	CISO must be experienced in governance and assessing risks to properly manage a security program and make the necessary adjustments based on the business risks the company is experiencing. Without an adequate GRC program, you cannot measure the effectiveness of your programs.
C	CISO ensures that all initiatives run smoothly and receive the funding they need. Ensure corporate leadership understands their role in Cyber Security. Securing adequate resources from the board of directors, the GRC aspect of CISO work is upwards focused in the org chart. Governance is slow and items which do not persist as risk register items for more than one quarter do not qualify as board-level governance concerns. Speaking at this executive level of management and compliance, the intent is to make sure that IT controls, finance controls and security controls are integrated and tracked holistically rather than in discrete business departments/functions

When asked "Which of these knowledge areas/experiences are critical for a Chief Information Security Officer (CISO)?", in the first focus group, three main items were identified (see Table 2). In the second focus group, most participants agreed that the first option is the best describer of the Governance, Risk and Compliance as a knowledge area/experience critical for a CISO.

Table 3. Results from Focus Groups - Question 2.2

Q	Which of these knowledge areas/experiences are critical for a Chief Information Security Officer (CISO)? Technical Knowledge and Skills
	Responses: A 4; B 2; C 1; D 0
A	CISO needs technical knowledge and skills to efficiently drive the technical strategy for tools and processes and balance the costs against the risk appetite of the organization. Tools are expensive. Features, APIs, system integration, automation, etc. need to be understood to manage change, people, and process.
B	Less important, since Cyber Security Teams have Security Analysts who are technical experts to work under the CISO. They follow the policies and procedures that were approved by the CISO. The CISO needs the ability to understand the technical aspects of security but not required to perform any security functions. player-coach as opposed to pure coach CISO profiles are finding their way into modern cybersecurity programs.
C	CISO is a hands-on role, with direct knowledge and participation in the tools and techniques of managing security across the organization. Real-time analysis of immediate threats, and triage.

When asked "Which of these knowledge areas/experiences are critical for a Chief Information Security Officer (CISO)?", in the first focus group, three main items were identified (see Table 3). In the second focus group, most participants agreed that the first option is the best describer of the Technical Knowledge and Skills as a knowledge area/experience critical for a CISO.

Table 4. Results from Focus Groups - Question 2.3

Q	Which of these knowledge areas/experiences are critical for a Chief Information Security Officer (CISO)? Managerial Experience
	Responses: A 2; B 2; C 3; D 0
A	Building great teams, mentoring, career, and education development, getting the most out of people while at the same time having them feel empowered and an appreciated member are skills required to be an effective CISO. Understanding skill gap, how to prioritize workloads and meeting business deadlines. Managerial experience is helpful to properly motivate his or her team in following the company's vision and mission around security.
B	Extremely important, if you cannot speak to senior management about the risks and why they need to adequately budget for security projects, then you cannot effectively perform your job. Management needs the confidence that you can supervise projects in a timely manner and within budget and communicate their benefits to management.

| C | CISOs need to be influencers and they are required to wear many hats within any organization regardless of its maturity, size or industry. For this aspect of the CISO's role to be effective, they must be able to switch between different types of conversations with any of their colleagues: executive, strategic and tactical. These types of discussions include executive, strategic, tactical, etc. |

When asked "Which of these knowledge areas/experiences are critical for a Chief Information Security Officer (CISO)?", in the first focus group, three main items were identified (see Table 4). In the second focus group, most participants agreed that the third option is the best describer of the Managerial Experience as a knowledge area/experience critical for a CISO.

Table 5. Results from Focus Groups - Question 3

Q	Which of these statements is most true?
	Responses: A 0; B 0; C 0; D 3; E 4
A	CISO needs to be able to manage relationships with vendors and negotiate terms that are favorable to the organization. CISOs need to provide feedback and encourage the vendor to implement features when needed.
B	CISO needs to engage with other CISOs in order to receive feedback and gage the progress of its own organization. CISO needs to have a trusted community of peers to discuss challenges they face and share ideas with to grow and learn how to continuously improve their organization's security

C	CISO needs to be familiar with the various frameworks in order to map control requirements against the controls of the organization
D	CISO need to focus on resilience. Resilience is more about what happens *after* the attack and how quickly you can get back up after being hit by an attack or a breach. And it's not like the engineering definition of resilience which might have to do with tensile strength or ductile properties of metallurgy. Resilience in the cyber definition should be about adaptation, robustness and transformation after being exposed to extreme conditions and forces (such as a DDoS attack or a ransomware outbreak).
E	CISO needs to engage thoughtful experimentation regarding defense capabilities in order to take a more active posture rather than passive approach to failure. Scheduling a tabletop exercise, pentest, red team exercise or threat hunting engagement is what can be called "active defense" so a team knows who might attack, when they might attack and what techniques they are most likely to use against you. Threat intelligence and continuous monitoring are two important ingredients when bringing into existence an active defense approach.

Five statements about the activities of CISOs were generated from the first focus group and the participants in the second focus group were asked to rate which of the five statements is most true about CISOs' activities (see Table 5). Most of the participants chose option four, then option three as the most accurate for CISO activities.

Table 6. Results from Focus Groups - Question 4

Q	What Certification(s), if any, should a Chief Information Security Officer (CISO) have?
	Responses: A 3; B 0; C 0; D 0: E 4
A	CISSP as it provides a measurement of understanding for the domains covered in the certification
B	CISM
C	CCISO
D	QTE Boardroom Readiness
E	Experiences is more important than certifications. I don't believe that certifications usually equate to being qualified If they have a support staff to assist in areas that are not their strengths, then they don't need any specific certifications

In the first focus group, five main CISO certifications were identified (see Table 6). In the second focus group, when asked "What Certification(s), if any, should a Chief Information Security Officer (CISO) have?", most participants agreed that the first and the fifth certifications are the main certifications that a CISO should have.

Table 7. Results from Focus Groups - Question 5.1

Q	What responsibility should each of the following have for Cyber Security Governance? Board of Directors
	Responses: A 0; B 6; C 1
A	Ensure that the executive team is prepared and has a plan for the eventuality of a cyber-attack. In addition, it is the boards responsibility to supporting the funding for the plan when agreed to.
B	Oversight of cybersecurity management and strategy. Ensuring that risk is understood from a legal and regulatory perspective.
C	BOD should hold the CISO and executive leadership responsible for Cyber Security. They should ask questions as needed to gain a better understanding of the Company's security posture

In the first focus group, the main responsibilities were identified for the Board of Directors (see Table 7). In the second focus group, when asked "What responsibility should each of the following have for Cyber Security Governance?", most participants agreed that the second option is the most accurate description of the responsibilities of the Board of Directors.

Table 8. Results from Focus Groups - Question 5.2

Q	What responsibility should each of the following have for Cyber Security Governance? Board of Trustees
	Responses: A 0; B 1; C 2; D4
A	Board of Trustees are responsible to make sure that the executive team is prepared and has a plan for the eventuality of a cyber-attack
B	Oversight of cybersecurity management and strategy. Ensuring that risk is understood from a legal and regulatory perspective.
C	Should hold the CISO and executive leadership responsible for Cyber Security. They should ask questions as needed to gain a better understanding of the Company's security posture
D	Ultimate accountability for making sure the organization has applied adequate resources to protecting the intellectual property of the business, the data of the customers and the integrity of the organization with respect to compliance and auditability for self-imposed as well as regulatory-imposed controls.

In the first focus group, the main responsibilities were identified for the Board of Trustees (see Table 8). In the second focus group, when asked "What responsibility should each of the following have for Cyber Security Governance?", most participants agreed that the fourth option is the most accurate description of the responsibilities of the Board of Trustees.

Table 9. Results from Focus Groups - Question 5.3

Q	What responsibility should each of the following have for Cyber Security Governance? Chief Information Security Officer (CISO)
	Responses: A 3; B 0; C 3; D 0; E1
A	Responsible for the Security Program
B	Build cyber framework according to CIA triad.
C	CISO is responsible for the strategy, budget and execution of the policies and procedures for Cyber Security Governance
D	Effective communication upwards, downwards and laterally within an organization.
E	CISO can be empowering a mindset of security by finding and rewarding "security champions" which are not among their direct reports. This is the area of "influence" when talking about embedding security into a company culture. It's this mindset that is important when building and managing modern cyber security governance at the program level.

In the first focus group, the main responsibilities were identified for CISOs (see Table 9). In the second focus group, when asked "What responsibility should each of the following have for Cyber Security Governance?", most participants agreed that the first and the third option is the most accurate description of the responsibilities of CISOs.

Table 10. Results from Focus Groups - Question 5.4

Q	What responsibility should each of the following have for Cyber Security Governance? Managers
	Responses: A 3; B 1; C 2; D 1
A	Responsible for supporting Cyber Security policies and the governance processes within their department.
B	Implementing the strategy, and communicating new or changing risks upwards to senior management
C	Responsible for implementing the Security Program. Managers internalize the pillars of infosec: availability, integrity, and confidentiality.
D	Managers have a significant role to play in effective governance

In the first focus group, the main responsibilities were identified for Managers (see Table 10). In the second focus group, when asked "What responsibility should each of the following have for Cyber Security Governance?", most participants agreed that the first option is the most accurate description of the responsibilities of Managers.

Table 11. Results from Focus Groups - Question 5.5

Q	What responsibility should each of the following have for Cyber Security Governance? Employees
	Responses: A 0; B 5; C 2
A	Employees are responsible for supporting policies.

B	Responsible for understanding and following the Security Program.
C	They must communicate risks.

In the first focus group, the main responsibilities were identified for Employees (see Table 11). In the second focus group, when asked "What responsibility should each of the following have for Cyber Security Governance?", most participants agreed that the second option is the most accurate description of the responsibilities of Employees.

Table 12. Results from Focus Groups - Question 6

Q	Which is most true?
	Responses: A 1; B 2; C 4
A	Contracts also play a role in cyber governance.
B	Third-party suppliers/partners must be aware of and follow established cybersecurity policies
C	Regulatory bodies are, in many cases, not keeping up with the times. The oversight of an industry should entail strong monitoring and enforcement of breach reporting.

Three statements about the third parties were generated from the first focus group and the participants in the second focus group were asked to rate which of the five statements is most true about third parties (see Table 12). Most of the participants chose the third option as the most accurate for third parties' involvement in cyber governance.

Table 13. Results from Focus Groups - Question 7

Q	How has Cyber Security Governance changed in the United States in the last 5 years?
	Responses: A 0; B 2; C 4; F 1
A	Governance has matured in the aspect of incorporating change management, vulnerability management
B	Increased focus on third-party risk management. Customers and clients have put the pressure on companies they do business with to have a formal information security program and to provide evidence like policies, MFA configurations, password policies, risk assessments, etc.
C	The board is starting to pay a closer attention to Cyber Security issues and concerns. There is a shift into greater awareness and more frequent participation of cybersecurity leadership in the overall governance functions of most companies. It is emerging from the technical weeds of IT and taking up a seat at the proverbial table
D	Regulators are starting to hold company leadership and boards responsible for security failures Boards and C-Suites recognize there is an added business risk and now seem to understand that expertise is needed at the table with the rest of the C-Suite to better understand and protected against the added risk. Leadership has taken an interest in truly defining their risk tolerance. CISOs are becoming key members of the executive leadership team.

E	Frameworks are being adopted. Policies are being implemented. Controls are being put in place, along with resiliency capabilities.
F	With more data being migrated to cloud services, there is a need for an understanding of how to govern data that is being hosted by a vendor. Cyber threats have gotten to be more severe and creative, so organization need to understand where their biggest risks are and be able to react to incidents quicker than they previously did.

When asked "How has Cyber Security Governance changed in the United States in the last 5 years?", in the first focus group, six main trends were identified (see Table 13). In the second focus group, most participants agreed that the third option is the most accurate statement for the changes in cyber security governance in the US.

Table 14. Results from Focus Groups - Question 8

Q	What is the most important aspect of Cyber Security Governance in your organization?
	Responses: A 0; B 1; C 4; D2
A	Vulnerability Management has become priority as new hacking groups emerge and more exploits are being known the wild and what it takes to remediate these findings in the organization
B	Establishing procedures that are audit ready, ensuring logs of systems are included in our log retention system for visibility, MFA is implemented when supported, and

	that the culture of the organization is changing with the process changes being introduced to support governance.
C	After so many years (or decades) of being a chaotic response-only effort, the development of well-defined program aligned to a well-respected framework is the current most important aspect.
D	Most important aspect of Governance is ensuring that our client's data is not compromised by an unauthorized user.
E	Regular reporting to the board of directors (each quarter at a minimum) and the corporate risk register exists, is reviewed regularly, contains board-level cybersecurity governance items.
F	The average score of our core vendors/service providers is tracked as a KPI

When asked "What is the most important aspect of Cyber Security Governance in your organization?", in the first focus group, six main aspects were identified (see Table 14). In the second focus group, most participants agreed that the third option is the most important aspect of Cyber Security Governance.

Table 15. Results from Focus Groups - Question 9

Q	What has changed in the role of a Chief Information Security Officer (CISO) in United States Organization in the last 5 years?
	Responses: A 0; B 2; C 2; D 2; E 1
A	CISO has become more of someone who is reporting to the board and overseeing the development of the security program. The CISO hires directors and manager in which whom takes on the responsibility to build the cyber framework and reduce risk within the organization
B	More requirements around technology skills for CISOs. Boards are seeing the need after experiencing breaches.
C	The biggest change has been the mindset shift of protecting the systems to protecting the 'data'. With the proliferation and adoption of third-party cloud services, the risk to the company data has significantly increased. CISOs must now communicate the risk to the data upwards. CISOs need to define and implement updated data protection controls and strategies
D	The CISO is more of an influencer today than they were 5 years ago. The CISO must influence the board to get funding to address key concerns. The CISO must influence his team to implement his\her plan to address the key concerns.
E	The average tenure at an organization is less than 18 months for a CISO in their position with a company. There is no meaningful answer to the question "are we secure?" when asked by an executive or board member.

	Executive team and C-Suite do not understand that a security program is a compromise between risk appetite, cost and agreeing on an acceptable level of "residual risk" for the organization.
F	We can transfer risk with cyber insurance or outsourcing of certain capabilities or functions of the company (like purchasing a virtual SOC instead of running an in-house team to monitor security alerts and events 24x7
G	CISOs are evolving from a deeply technical role towards a more "risk management" role. Some CISOs retain that technical depth, but in addition they are adopting a more high-level approach to risk. Think perhaps of the meaning implied by evolving from simple risk management towards "risk intelligence" and taking an approach that is intent on solving problems of scale with automation and orchestration.

When asked "What has changed in the role of a Chief Information Security Officer (CISO) in United States Organization in the last 5 years?", in the first focus group, seven main trends were identified (see Table 15). In the second focus group, most participants agreed that the second, third, and fourth option is the most accurate statement for the changes in the role of CISOs in the US in the past 5 years.

Table 16. Results from Focus Groups - Question 10

Q	Do you think the role of the Chief Information Security Officer (CISO) will change in the next 5 years?
	Responses: A 0; B 3; C 1; D 2; E1
A	No not in the next 5 years but in the future as our technology expands to incorporate future technology such as block chain, crypto and cloud.
B	Yes, there will be continuing change for technology skills requirements as well as CISOs leading IT Infrastructure due to the security requirements across infrastructure and cloud.
C	Yes, the CISO role will continue evolve. With the average lifespan of a CISO role to about 2 years. A CISO needs to evolve in their role or risk being obsolete to meet the demands of the role and business requirements that are always changing and evolving.
D	Yes, CISO will have more accountability and be more compliance oriented.
E	They will need to be more diligent about tracking and reporting even the smallest cyber event.

When asked "Do you think the role of the Chief Information Security Officer (CISO) will change in the next 5 years?", in the first focus group, five main trends were identified (see Table 16). In the second focus group, most participants agreed that the second option is the most accurate statement for the expected changes in the role of CISOs in the US in the next 5 years.

Table 17. Results from Focus Groups - Question 11

Q	What is a critical question relating to the Role of the Chief Information Security Officer (CISO)?
	Responses: A 0; B 3; C 4
A	Why when a breach occurs the CISO is the first to go? To a CISOs defense he/she is just one person who may or may not have limited staff and has got the communication to the board that in cyber there is no silver bullet.
B	Why is CISO turnover so high? Burnout?
C	What are some of the challenges to communicating upwards for CISOs (e.g. risk education)?
D	What is the path to CISO in terms of training, college major and career titles that led to the role?
E	What is the value of a CISO reaching this role by "the path less travelled" instead of a CISOs that were former computer science students/graduates?

When asked "What is a critical question relating to the Role of the Chief Information Security Officer (CISO)?", in the first focus group, five main aspects were identified (see Table 17). In the second focus group, most participants agreed that the third option is the most accurate statement for the question relating to the Role of the CISO.

Part 2: The General Survey

Following the findings from the Focus Group research, the second part of the research comprised of a multiple-choice survey that was filled by anonymously 90 Cyber Security Managers.

Initial Contact with Survey Participants

A letter (see Appendices section) was sent to CISOs and posted on LinkedIn. It was also shared by Cyber Security Collaboration Forum to Leadership Board Members, CDO Magazine to some select CISOs, and NYISC2 Chapter to members.

General Survey Responses

Below are presented the results from the responses acquired from the general survey.

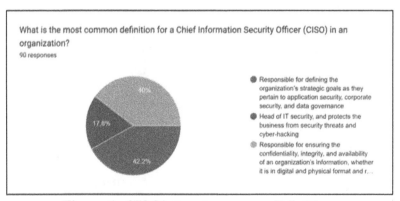

Figure 1. CISO's most common definition

The definition most selected (42.5%) was that the CISO is responsible for the organization's strategic goals. A close second (42%) was they are responsible for confidentiality, integrity, and availability of information. The least selected

(17.8%) was they are the head of IT and they protect the business from security threats and cyber-hacking.

The top 2 definitions suggest that the CISO is responsible for confidentiality, integrity and availability of information while meeting the organization's strategic goas, at least as far as Information/Cyber Security is concerned.

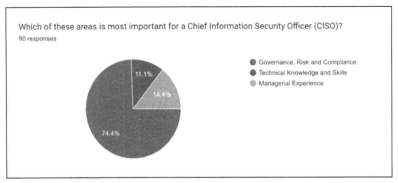

Figure 2. CISO most important areas

74.4% responded that Governance, Risk and Compliance are most important for a CISO. Followed by 14.4% who responded managerial experience and 11.1% who responded technical knowledge and skills.

This demonstrates how critical Governance, Risk and Compliance are in relation to Information/Cyber Security.

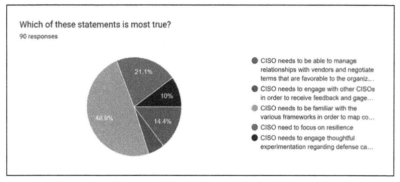

Figure 3. CISO's activity

The statement deemed most true (48.9%) was that a CISO needs to be familiar with the various frameworks to map control requirements against the organization's controls. The second most true statement (21.1%) was the need to focus on resilience. The next three selected were the need to be able to manage relationships with vendors and negotiate terms that are favorable to the organization (14.4%) and CISO needs to engage in thoughtful experimentation regarding defense capabilities (10%). Finally, the last category that they need to engage with other CISOs only received (5.6%).

Organizations may have to comply with ISO, HIPAA, PCI, GDPR and others. Therefore, it seems appropriate that mapping control requirements against the controls of the organization was selected by 48.9%.

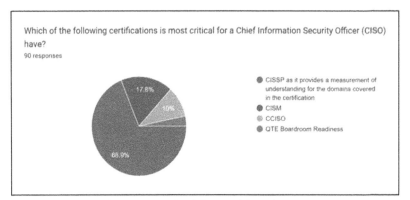

Figure 4. CISO certifications

CISSP received (68.9%) of the responses, as it provides a measurement of understanding for the domains covered in the certification. The next two categories, CISM (17.8%) and CCISO (10%), received some responses. The least favorite choice was QTE Boardroom Readiness, which only received 3.3% of the responses.

Many open positions on LinkedIn state that CISSP is a requirement. Based on the selection of CISSP by 68.9%, organizations requiring this certification of a CISO believe it provides a measurement of understanding of the areas that a CISO should know.

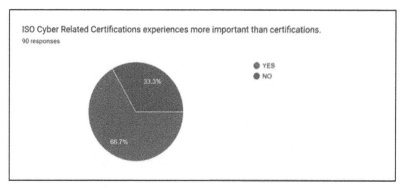

Figure 5. Importance of ISO certifications for CISOs

66.7% vs. 33.3% of the respondents believed ISO Certifications were more important than the certifications in the previous question. 66.7% believe that having ISO Certifications is more important than other certifications. While CISSP provides a measurement of understanding for the domains covered in the certification, ISO Certifications require not only knowledge but also experience in implementing each certification area in which they are certified. There are over 22,600 different ISO standards in which an individual can be certified.

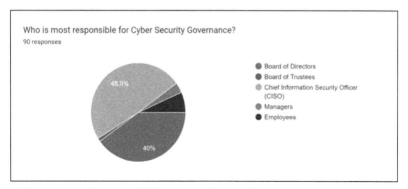

Figure 6. Responsibility for Cyber Security Governance

The respondents' reference as to who is most responsible for Cyber Security Governance were Chief Information Security Office (49.9%) followed by the Board of Directors (40%). The remaining responses which made up the remaining (10.1%) in orders were about employees, managers, and Board of Trustees.

The fact that 49.9% chose the CISO as most responsible for Governance, reinforces the response to the previous question relating to the responsibilities of a CISO, where Governance, Risk and Compliance were selected as the top area for a CISO.

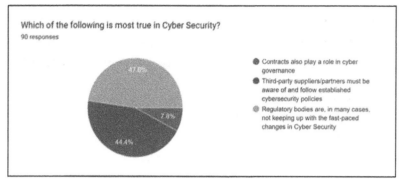

Figure 7. Cyber Security Governance

As far as which statement was most true, the responses for the top two were very close with regulatory bodies are, in many cases, not keeping up with the fast-paced changes in Cyber Security receiving 47.8%) of the responses, followed by third-party suppliers/partners must be aware of and follow established cybersecurity policies (44.4%). The last choice selected was that Contracts also play a role in cyber governance (7.8%).

Regulatory bodies are not keeping up with the fast-paced changes, according to the response of 47.8%. This ties in with requirements that Third Party Vendors must comply with per regulations. If regulatory bodies are not keeping up, this could mean that requirements for Third Party Vendors are not up to date either.

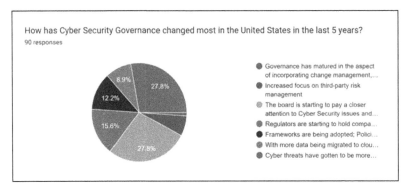

Figure 8. Changes in Cyber Security Governance

There was a tie between Cyber threats have gotten to be more severe and creative, so organization need to understand where their biggest risks are and be able to react to incidents quicker than they previously did (27.8%) and the board is starting to pay a closer attention to Cyber Security issues and concerns (27.8%). The next highest response was regulators are starting to hold company leadership and boards responsible for security failures Boards (15.6%). The least selected choices were frameworks are being adopted, policies are being implemented, and controls are being put in place, along with resiliency capabilities (12.2%) and with more data being migrated to cloud services, there is a need for an understanding of how to govern data that is being hosted by a vendor (8.9%). Risk assessments are going to be critical to keep up with new risks and respond.

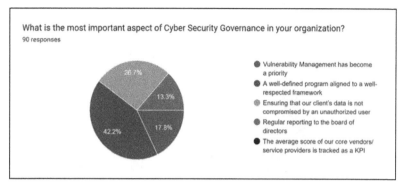

Figure 9. Important aspects of Cyber Security Governance

The most important aspect of Cyber Security Governance in the respondent's organizations was a well-defined program aligned to a well-respected framework (42.2%). Followed by ensuring that client's data is not compromised by an unauthorized user (26.7%), vulnerability Management has become a priority (17.8%) and finally, regular reporting to the board of directors (13.3%).

Based on the responses, a well-respected framework is needed to govern against, which in turn will require controls to protect against compromise and for vulnerability management. The implementation of the controls and metrics should be reported to the board of directors.

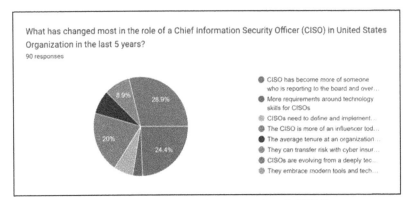

Figure 10. Changes in the role of CISOs

The top responses refence to what has changed most in the role of a Chief Information Security Officer (CISO) in United States Organization in the last 5 years was close, all within the 20th percentile range. Most respondents chose more requirements around technology skills for CISOs (28.9%) followed by CISO has become more of someone who is reporting to the board and overseeing the development of the security program (24.4%), and the CISO is more of an influencer today than they were 5 years ago (20%). Only 8.9% chose that they can transfer risk with cyber insurance or outsourcing of certain capabilities or functions of the company (like purchasing a virtual SOC instead of running an in-house team to monitor security alerts and events 24x7). The last four selected options shared the bottom 17.8% and were: the average tenure at an organization is less than 18 months for a CISO in their position with a company; CISOs need to define and implement updated data protection controls and strategies; more requirements around technology skills for CISOs; and they embrace modern tools and techniques for mitigating all tiers of vendors.

The responses show that both technical skills and overseeing the development of the security program while reporting to the board are the main changes in the last five years.

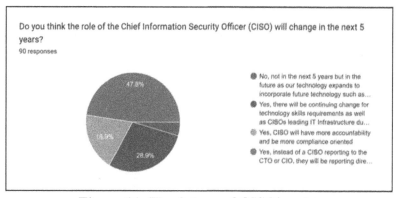

Figure 11. The future of CISO's role

Regarding to the role of the Chief Information Security Officer (CISO) changing in the next 5 years, almost half of the respondents selected that instead of a CISO reporting to the CTO or CIO, they will be reporting directly to the CEO (Chief Risk Officer) if one exists (47.8%). 28.9% believe that there will be continuing change for technology skills requirements as well as CISOs leading IT Infrastructure due to the security requirements across infrastructure and cloud. 18.9% believe CISOs will have more accountability and be more compliance oriented. Only 4.4% do not believe that the role of the CISO will change in the next 5 years but that it will in the future as technology expands to incorporate future technology such as blockchain, crypto and cloud.

Based on the top two results, CISOs will be reporting directly to the CRO (Chief Risk Officer) if one exists and the CISO will need to keep up their knowledge and technology skills requirements while leading IT Infrastructure due to the security requirements across infrastructure and cloud.

Summary of Research results

This subchapter summarizes what has been generally agreed upon by the Focus Group and Mass survey respondents.

A common definition for a Chief Information Security Officer (CISO) in an organization is, a CISO is responsible for defining its strategic goals as they pertain to application security, corporate security, and data governance. The CISO sets the vision for its enterprise security strategy with a clear roadmap and work closely with its leadership team across Engineering, Product, IT, and Compliance to make sure the roadmap is executed. They create, implement, and maintain a security team, build on existing security policies, procedures, standards, and guidelines, and work with customers and prospects to address security concerns. Responsible for developing and implementing an information security program which entails day to day operations, which includes strategy development.

A CISO needs technical knowledge and skills to efficiently drive the technical strategy for tools and processes and balance the costs against the risk appetite of the organization. Tools are expensive. System integration, automation, etc. need to be understood to manage change, people, and process. CISOs need to be influencers and they are required to wear many hats within any organization regardless of its maturity, size or industry. For this aspect of the CISO's role to be effective, they must be able to switch between different types of conversations with any of their colleagues: executive, strategic and tactical. These types of discussions include executive, strategic, tactical, etc.

CISO needs to engage thoughtful experimentation regarding defense capabilities in order to take a more active posture rather than passive approach to failure. Scheduling a tabletop exercise, pentest, red team exercise or threat hunting engagement is what can be called "active defense" so a team knows who might attack, when they might attack and what techniques they are most likely to use against you. Threat intelligence and continuous monitoring are two important ingredients when bringing into existence an active defense approach. A CISO needs to be familiar with the various frameworks to map control requirements against the organization's controls.

Experiences is more important than certifications. Certifications usually equate to being qualified If they have a support staff to assist in areas that are not their strengths, then they do not need any specific certifications. However, CISSP certification provides a measurement of understanding for the domains covered in the certification. ISO Certifications are more important than a CISSP certification. A CISO is responsible for the oversight of cybersecurity management and strategy. They must ensure that risk is understood from a legal and regulatory perspective.

The Board of Trustees has ultimate accountability for making sure the organization has applied adequate resources to protecting the intellectual property of the business, the data of the customers and the integrity of the organization with respect to compliance and auditability for self-imposed as well as regulatory-imposed controls. The board is starting to pay a closer attention to Cyber Security issues and concerns. There is a shift into greater awareness and more frequent participation of cybersecurity leadership in the overall governance functions of most companies. It is emerging from the technical weeds of IT and taking up a seat at the proverbial table.

Cyber threats have gotten to be more severe and creative, so organization need to understand where their biggest risks are and be able to react to incidents quicker than they previously did. The board is starting to pay a closer attention to Cyber Security issues and concerns. There are more requirements around technology skills for CISOs. The CISO has become more of s someone who is reporting to the board and overseeing the development of the security program.

Most important aspect of Governance is ensuring that an unauthorized user does not compromise the client's data. Regulatory bodies are, in many cases, not keeping up with the times. The oversight of an industry should entail strong monitoring and enforcement of breach reporting. The most important aspect of Cyber Security Governance in the respondent's organizations was a well-defined program aligned to a well-respected framework.

Governance, Risk and Compliance are most important for a CISO. CISO's are responsible for supporting Cyber Security policies and the governance processes within their department.

Employees are responsible for understanding and following the Security Program.

CISO is responsible for the strategy, budget and execution of the policies and procedures for Cyber Security Governance. They can empower a mindset of security by finding and rewarding "security champions" which are not among their direct reports. This is the area of "influence" when talking about embedding security into a company culture. It is this mindset that is important when building and managing modern cyber security governance at the program level.

Some the changes in the last five years have been there are more requirements around technology skills for CISOs. Boards are seeing the need after experiencing breaches. The biggest change has been the mindset shift of protecting the systems to protecting the 'data.' With the proliferation and adoption of third-party cloud services, the risk to the company data has significantly increased. CISOs must now communicate the risk to the data upwards. CISOs need to define and implement updated data protection controls and strategies.

In the next five years is there will be continuing change for technology skills requirements as well as CISOs leading IT Infrastructure due to the security requirements across infrastructure and cloud. instead of a CISO reporting to the CTO or CIO, they will be reporting directly to the CEO (Chief Risk Officer) if one exists.

Conclusions and Recommendations

Research Question 1

How is Cyber Security governed within organizations within the United States?

The CISO is also in charge of monitoring and responding to data breaches, as well as keeping track of new security threats and vulnerabilities. It's the responsibility of the CISO to stay up to date with the latest advances in cyber security and make sure that their organization has an adequate level of protection against any potential attacks. Additionally, effective communication between the Board, CISO, and other stakeholders is essential in order to ensure a successful governance program. The Board of Directors is ultimately responsible for governance and information security in a company. However, having the right policies and tools in place to ensure cyber security is the responsibility of the Chief Information Security Officer (CISO).

The CISO must take appropriate measures to secure sensitive data, as well as create and maintain all necessary policies, processes and procedures that are required for an effective governance program. The development of policies and procedures should be based on industry best practices and adapted to meet specific needs of the organization. All processes and protocols should be regularly updated to reflect new technologies or potential changes in risk levels within the company. This can include everything from patch management, threat intelligence gathering and analysis, incident response.

Research Question 1.2

Who is responsible for the governance, risk and compliance of Information and Cyber Security withing the organization?

Governance risk and compliance for information and cyber security within an organization are typically the responsibility of the Chief Information Security Officer (CISO). The CISO is responsible for establishing, implementing, and managing the organization's security framework. The CISO may be tasked with ensuring that all employees are following security policies and procedures, as well as selecting and implementing appropriate solutions to protect the organization's data. They may also be responsible for creating training programs to ensure their workforce is properly educated on cybersecurity-related topics.

In addition to the role of the CISO, there may be other senior personnel within the organization who are responsible for overseeing governance risk and compliance for information and cyber security. These individuals may include legal counsel or heads of departments or divisions such as finance, human resources, or marketing. When it comes to cyber security, organizations must also consider the impact of external threat actors. It is important that they be vigilant in monitoring their IT infrastructure and data for signs of malicious activities or unauthorized access.

In order to ensure that governance risk and compliance for information and cyber security are properly managed, organizations should have a comprehensive set of tools and procedures in place to identify potential risks, vulnerabilities, and threats. Organizations should also employ appropriate measures to mitigate any existing or potential risks. It is important for organizations to have a unified vision when it comes to governance risk and compliance for information and cyber security. This means that all departments should be working together to ensure that the organization is adhering to established standards and protocols in this area.

Organizations should invest in staff training to ensure that all employees understand the importance of cyber security and are aware of their roles and responsibilities when it comes to managing governance risk and compliance for information and cyber security within the organization.

Research Question 2

What role do the Boards of Directors play in the Governance of Cyber Security?

Cyber security is an increasingly important subject for organizations, and the board of directors plays a critical role in governing it. The board of directors is responsible for setting policies and procedures that protect company data and systems from cyber threats. By doing so, they ensure that all members of the organization remain compliant with industry standards and best practices. The board must also be aware of the current trends in cyber security and review them regularly to stay up to date on new threats. They should also research other companies' cyber security policies to gain insight into best practices. The board must have clear plans for responding to any incidents or breaches that occur, as well as for developing preventive measures against future occurrences.

Another major responsibility of the board of directors when it comes to cybersecurity is providing guidance on investments in technology, personnel and training. This includes reviewing existing budgets and making suggestions for upgrades or additional resources if necessary. Additionally, the board should assist in evaluating proposed solutions for different types of cyber security threats and deciding which ones will best suit the organization's needs. Regular monitoring should also be done to track progress towards achieving desired outcomes from these efforts. The board of directors also serves as a resource for the organization when it comes to cyber security. They should review and understand the implications of any new policies being proposed in order to properly assess their efficacy and any possible risks that may arise from implementing them. Additionally, the board should regularly evaluate vendors providing services or products related to cyber security and make sure they are adequately meeting the organization's needs.

It is important for the board to be aware of potential legal implications around data privacy and cyber-related violations. They must ensure legal compliance with national laws and regulations regarding consumer data protection, privacy standards for employee data, as well as any other applicable laws related to cyber security. By taking all these measures into account, organizations can develop sensible strategies that protect their data from breaches while remaining compliant with both local and international regulation.

The board should ensure there are sufficient internal controls in place that address potential areas of concern related to cyber security. This may include establishing processes to audit access rights, creating guidelines around acceptable user activity, educating employees on how to spot suspicious behavior online, and having contingency plans ready in case of a breach or attack. In summary, ensuring organizations are adequately protected against cyber threats requires regular oversight by the board of directors. They must evaluate changing trends in technology and make sure strategies are being sufficiently implemented across the organization while adhering to industry standards and best practices. By taking a proactive approach towards cybersecurity governance, organizations can reduce their vulnerabilities.

Research Question 3 - What role does the Chief Information Security Officer have in Cyber Security Governance?

The Chief Information Security Officer (CISO) is a pivotal role within any organization's governance system. As the head of a company's IT security team, the individual in this position is tasked with developing and maintaining secure systems to protect sensitive data, as well as managing any incidents or threats that arise. The CISO must also ensure compliance with industry regulations and standards, such as HIPAA and GDPR.

When it comes to governance, the role of the CISO is two-fold. On one hand, they are responsible for ensuring that IT systems are properly secured and regularly updated to remain compliant with applicable laws and regulations. This involves creating policies and procedures around access control, user authentication, data encryption, patch management, auditing and logging. On the other hand, they must work closely with all departments within an organization to provide training on cyber security protocols, identify potential vulnerabilities, support incident response efforts when needed, and coordinate with third-party vendors who may have access to sensitive data.

In order to be successful in their profession, CISOs must possess an intricate understanding of IT infrastructure as well as a deep knowledge of various technologies such as cloud computing and virtualization. They must also stay current pn standards and trends in information security practices and have strong leadership skills to effectively manage their team. The ideal candidate for this position should have extensive experience in IT risk management and be able to demonstrate a proven track record of protecting confidential data from malicious actors.

Overall, having an experienced CISO who is dedicated solely to managing the company's cyber security is essential for proper governance today given the ever increasing number of cyber threats arising from sophisticated hackers or "bad actors" who seek out weaknesses in systems by targeting vulnerabilities or disregarding privileged access.. When implemented correctly, these measures will not only help mitigate risks but will ultimately result in better information availability through improved performance while increasing customer satisfaction by strengthening trust within your enterprise architecture.

Research Question 3.1 - What skills and certifications should CISO's acquire to be most effective?

A Chief Information Security Officer (CISO) needs to have a range of skills and expertise such as:

- Technical expertise: A CISO needs an in-depth knowledge of a wide range of security topics, including cryptography, network security, software design, authentication protocols and cyber defense. It is essential for them to understand the technical aspects of computer networks, as well as how different technologies interact with each other.
- Risk management experience: One of the main duties of a CISO is risk management. They must assess areas where the organization could be vulnerable, identify potential threats and develop strategies to mitigate any risks. In addition, they need to be able to communicate these risks effectively with stakeholders so that proper action can be taken.
- Leadership abilities: Leading an information security team requires strong leadership skills. The CISO should have the ability to motivate their team members and ensure everyone is working together towards a shared goal. They also need excellent problem-solving skills

and the ability to make quick decisions in critical situations.

- Communication skills: An effective CISO should also have excellent communication skills. Not only do they need to be able to explain complex security concepts in simple language, they should also have exceptional interpersonal skills so they can explain their strategies and ideas clearly and concisely.

Certification in international standards related to IT Governance, Risk Management, Information Security, and Cloud Security is important for several reasons. Each ISO Standard has been accepted and adopted by over 167 countries worldwide. No single certification is mandatory for all CISOs, but certifications can be beneficial in proving the necessary knowledge and experience to lead the cybersecurity field. Cybersecurity certifications are important for organizations to maintain security standards related to data privacy and information security. Some examples of relevant cybersecurity certifications include ISO/IEC 27001 Information Security Management System, ISO/IEC 27002 Information Security Controls, ISO/IEC 27005 Information Security Risk Management, ISO/IEC 27032 Lead Cybersecurity Manager, ISO/IEC 27035 Incident Management, ISO/IEC 27701 Security Techniques for Privacy Information Management, Lead Cloud Security Manager (covering both ISO/IEC 27017 and ISO/IEC 27018) and CISSP: Certified Information Systems Security Professional.

A CISO who is certified in applicable ISO Standards can can better assist an organization in adhering to accepted standards of practice and puts their cybersecurity measures on the same level as other businesses around the world. By certifying in International Standards (ISO), the CISO can assist the organization in leveraging the latest best practices for cyber defense. In addition, the CISSP certification demonstrates that the holder has mastered a comprehensive body of knowledge related to the aspect of risk management, cybersecurity, and IT. The survey participants rated ISO standards as more important, but that is important to have. CISSP as it provides a measurement of understanding for the domains covered in the certification.

A CISO who is certified in ISO Standards or CISSP is provided recognition that is respected across the globe and opens opportunities in major technology companies. Having this certification is also advantageous when it comes to salary negotiations and job promotion as it is a widely recognized credential that employers respect. Additionally, having either Certifications such as ISO and CISSP certification signifies that the individual has dedicated time and effort to develop their understanding of IT security operations and management, while also providing them with access to the latest industry practices.

Research Question 3.2 - What should a CISO be responsible for? What is a true definition of a CISO?

The role of the Chief Information Security Officer (CISO) in information and cyber governance has become vastly more important over the past five years. The rise of digital technology has created an environment where organizations are at risk of data breaches, malware attacks, and other threats to their sensitive information. This has led to an increased need for professionals who specialize in keeping these organizations secure from external threats. The primary responsibility of a CISO is to ensure that organizational information is being managed securely, as well as making sure that any sensitive data is being properly protected against malicious actors. In addition, CISOs are also responsible for educating staff on how to handle confidential data safely, instituting best practices and processes for security incidents when they occur, and creating policies that help align organizational goals with security objectives.

The need for competent CISOs has become even greater over the past five years due to the emergence of new cyber threats and technologies as well as changing regulations such as GDPR. For example, it is much more difficult today than ever before to protect personal data from malicious actors and protect it against disclosure without proper authorization. As a result, many organizations have hired independent experts or dedicated personnel to handle their security needs rather than relying on internal staff alone. In response to this increased demand for qualified individuals, the number of training programs specifically designed for CISOs has been steadily growing over the past few years. These specialized courses often cover topics such as incident response planning, compliance requirements like GDPR or PCI-DSS, threat intelligence management & analysis techniques, cryptography & system architecture principles and so on. Ultimately, having a well-trained and experienced individual managing security operations helps organizations stay ahead of emerging cyber threats and quickly address any potential issues that may arise – something which will only become increasingly important in coming years.

A Chief Information Security Officer (CISO) is an essential member of any organization's cyber security governance team. A CISO can provide the expertise, experience and insights to ensure effective information and cyber security is maintained throughout an organization. Here are five reasons why a CISO should be involved in information and cyber security governance:

1. Risk Management – A CISO is responsible for understanding the risks that come with different types of security threats and data breaches, as well as how to address them quickly and effectively. This allows organizations to respond quickly to emerging threats, reduce their potential impact and avoid unnecessary losses or expenditures.

2. Compliance – To keep up with changing regulations, laws, best practices or industry standards relating to information security, a CISO should be actively involved in making sure that measures are taken to meet all applicable requirements. This keeps an organization from getting fined or facing other penalties from regulatory bodies.

3. Policy Development – An experienced CISO has the necessary knowledge for developing policies that ensure effective information security protocols are in place for all aspects of an organization's operations. Such policies also need to be regularly updated as new technologies or threats emerge, which requires a comprehensive understanding of the most up-to-date solutions available on the market today.

4. Data Security Education– Employees must remain aware of the latest threats, best practices and procedures related to data security for any organized effort to succeed in keeping data secure at all times. A competent CISO is charged with training employees on such matters, so they understand the importance of following proper protocol when it comes to protecting critical information assets.

5. Vendor Oversight – It's important for any organization to know who can access their sensitive systems, data and materials at any given time during business operations; this means having complete control over third-party vendors that may have access rights over certain parts of an organization's network infrastructure or sensitive data stores — something only a knowledgeable CISO can ensure happens flawlessly under his/her watchful eye.

In five years, it is expected that the role of CISO will become even more significant; they must not only provide support but also demonstrate positive outcomes in terms of business objectives and customer satisfaction. To do this, CISOs must stay up to date on advances in technology, understanding customer needs and regulations, as well as having strong leadership capabilities.

Research Question 3.3 - To whom should the CISO report to?

In recent years, a focus on integrating safety and security with executive roles has led to an increase in the number of Chief Information Security Officers (CISOs) with a reporting line straight to the CEO. This reflects the importance of cybersecurity and its evolution from an IT-focused role to one essential for businesses. Having a CISO who reports directly to the CEO can improve strategic direction and communication between the cybersecurity team and other departments, enabling everyone to comply with security measures while reducing risk management costs. Cybersecurity is an increasingly important aspect of businesses in today's digital world. In order to ensure that organizations are safe from malicious cyber-attacks, they need a Chief Information Security Officer (CISO) to oversee security operations. However, there has been some debate as to who this CISO should report to. Some argue that the CISO should report exclusively to the Chief Information Officer (CIO). Others suggest that the CISO should report directly to either the CEO or board instead.

The research shows that in five years or before, the CISO will report to either the CEO or board instead of exclusively reporting to the CIO.

- The Mission of The CIO Differs from the Mission of the CISO: While both roles involve technology, their goals and objectives are different. While the CIO focuses on implementing new technologies, improving existing systems and processes, and maintaining uptime of applications, a key goal of a CISO is protecting systems and data from external threats and vulnerabilities. Having different chains of command allows these two objectives to remain distinct and uncompromised.

- Increased Autonomy for the CISO: If the CISOs reports directly either to the CEO or board, it increases their authority—instead of waiting for approval from their CIO supervisor for certain changes, they can go straight to those at the top if needed. This helps with decision-making and allows them greater autonomy in addressing cybersecurity concerns quickly and decisively.

- Greater Oversight: By having a separate chain of command, outside stakeholders such as directors on the board can be informed about cybersecurity issues without having any direct conflict with CIOs agendas or opinions on IT matters. Board members don't always have technical proficiency, but they can still be up to date on what's happening in terms of security since they will be informed by their company's own expert on said matters—the CISO!

While currently the CISO's usually work under a CIO's supervision, it remains generally more advantageous for them to have a separate channel of communication with either the

CEO or board depending on organizational needs. Doing so gives them increased autonomy in keeping organizations secure, while also guaranteeing higher levels of oversight from those at top management levels who may not have technical expertise but still need regular updates about current security operations within an organization

Bibliography

Agle, A. and Agle, A. (2008) *Information Security Governance: Centralized vs. Distributed | CSO Online, Www-csoonline-com.cdn.ampproject.org*. CSOONLINE. Available at: https://www-csoonline-com.cdn.ampproject.org/c/s/www.csoonline.com/article/2123153/information-security-governance--centralized-vs--distributed.amp.html (Accessed: 2020).

American Institute of Banking -Banking Topic Cyber Security (2021) *American Bankers Association*. American Bankers Association. Available at: http:///banking-topics/technology/cybersecurity (Accessed: 2021).

AUER, M.A.R.K.U.S. (2021) *How to Effectively Manage Cyber Threats on Critical Infrastructure, ThreatQuotient*. ThreatQuotient. Available at: https://www.threatq.com/effectively-manage-cyber-threats-critical-infrastructure/ (Accessed: 2021).

Baer, G. *et al.* (2021) *A Tower of Babel: Cyber Regulation for Financial Services | The Clearing House, Theclearinghouse.org*. THe Clearing House. Available at: https://www.theclearinghouse.org/banking-perspectives/2017/2017-q2-banking-perspectives/articles/cyber-regulation-for-financial-services (Accessed: 2021).

Bowen, M. (2022) *How security and business continuity became inseparable*, *Intelligent CISO*. Intelligent CISO. Available at: https://www.intelligentciso.com/2022/06/20/how-security-and-business-continuity-became-inseparable/ (Accessed: January 19, 2023).

Brooks, C. (2020) *The Cybersecurity Imperative of Protecting Critical Infrastructure - CyberTheory*, *CyberTheory*. Cyber Theory. Available at: https://cybertheory.io/the-cybersecurity-imperative-of-protecting-critical-infrastructure/ (Accessed: 2021).

Correia, J. (2022) *Where Does Risk Management Fit in with CISOs - Why Is It So Important?*, *TuxCare*. TuxCare. Available at: https://tuxcare.com/where-does-risk-management-fit-in-with-cisos-why-is-it-so-important/ (Accessed: January 16, 2023).

Cyber Security Jobs (2023) *Chief Information Security Officer (CISO) Jobs*, *Cyber Security Jobs*. Available at: https://www.cybersecurityjobs.com/chief-information-security-officer-jobs/ (Accessed: January 16, 2023).

Cybersecurity | American Bankers Association (2020) *Aba.com*. American Bankers Association. Available at: https://www.aba.com/banking-topics/technology/cybersecurity (Accessed: 2020).

Deloitte (2019) *Protecting against the Changing Cybersecurity Risk Landscape*, *Deloitte United States.*

Deloitte United States. Available at: https://www2.deloitte.com/us/en/pages/advisory/articles/ advanced-cyber-threats.html (Accessed: January 17, 2023).

Doyle, E. (2022) *How to understand the evolution of the CISO Role, CyberTalk*. Cyber Talk. Available at: https://www.cybertalk.org/2022/06/05/how-to-understand-the-evolution-of-the-ciso-role/ (Accessed: September 8, 2022).

Eisenbach, T.M., Kovner, A. and Lee, M.J. (2020) *Cyber Risk and the U.S. Financial System: A Pre-Mortem Analysis*. New York: Federal Reserve Bank of New York. Available at: https://www.newyorkfed.org/medialibrary/media/researc h/staff_reports/sr909.pdf (Accessed: 2020).

FFIEC (2016) *FFIEC IT Handbook Information Security Booklet*. US Government: Federal Financial Institutions Examination Council. Available at: https://www.ffiec.gov/press/PDF/FFIEC_IT_Handbook_ Information_Security_Booklet.pdf (Accessed: 2020).

Fruhlinger, J. (2021) *What Is a CISO? Responsibilities and Requirements for This Vital Role, CSO Online*. CSO. Available at: https://www.csoonline.com/article/3332026/what-is-a-ciso-responsibilities-and-requirements-for-this-vital-leadership-role.html (Accessed: January 17, 2023).

Fruhlinger, J. (2021) *What is a ciso? responsibilities and requirements for this vital role*, CSO Online. CSO. Available at: https://www.csoonline.com/article/3332026/what-is-a-ciso-responsibilities-and-requirements-for-this-vital-leadership-role.html (Accessed: May 5, 2022).

Gorge, M. (2022) *Author post: What is the role of a CISO in compliance?*, *Forbes*. Forbes Magazine. Available at: https://www.forbes.com/sites/forbesbooksauthors/2022/09/09/what-is-the-role-of-a-ciso-in-compliance/?sh=51429da31ce4 (Accessed: January 19, 2023).

Harner, C. *et al.* (2020) *Cyberattacks Could Cripple Major U.S. Banks*, *CFO*. CFO Magazine. Available at: https://www.cfo.com/cyber-security-technology/2020/03/cyberattacks-could-cripple-u-s-banking-system/ (Accessed: 2020).

Holmes , R. (2022) *A modern CISO's critical roles & responsibilities*, *Cyber Risk Analytics & Security Ratings*. BItSight. Available at: https://www.bitsight.com/blog/ciso-roles-and-responsibilities (Accessed: January 7, 2023).

Hughes, C. (2022) *Why CISOs Must be Part of Data Governance*, *Acceleration Economy*. Acceleration Economy Network. Available at: https://accelerationeconomy.com/cybersecurity/why-cisos-must-be-part-of-data-governance/ (Accessed: January 12, 2023).

Institute of World Politics (2020) *Evolution of the chief information security officer, Institute of World Politics.* The Institute of World Politics. Available at: https://cyberintelligence.world/evolution-of-the-chief-information-security-officer/#:~:text=In%201995%20a%20new%20executive,infrastructures%20upon%20which%20corporations%20relied. (Accessed: May 16, 2022).

ISO (2022) *ISO/IEC 27001 and related standards - information security management, ISO.* International Standards Organization . Available at: https://www.iso.org/isoiec-27001-information-security.html#:~:text=ISO%2FIEC%2027001%20is%20the,the%20ISO%2FIEC%2027000%20family. (Accessed: November 16, 2022).

Kaplan, J., Toomey, C. and Tyra, A. (2019) *Critical Resilience: Adapting Infrastructure to Repel Cyberthreats, McKinsey & Company.* McKinsey & Company. Available at: https://www.mckinsey.com/industries/travel-logistics-and-infrastructure/our-insights/critical-resilience-adapting-infrastructure-to-repel-cyberthreats (Accessed: 2021).

Kaplan, J., Toomey, C. and Tyra, A. (2020) *Critical resilience: Adapting infrastructure to repel cyberthreats,*

McKinsey & Company. McKinsey & Company.
Available at:
https://www.mckinsey.com/industries/travel-logistics-and-infrastructure/our-insights/critical-resilience-adapting-infrastructure-to-repel-cyberthreats (Accessed: January 18, 2023).

Katz, S.R. (2019) *Content by Stephen R. Katz, CISSP, Bank Information Security.* Available at:
https://www.bankinfosecurity.com/authors/stephen-r-katz-cissp-i-127 (Accessed: August 5, 2022).

Kemper, M. (2020) *Security Issues Relating to Internet Banking, AZ Central Part of USA Today Network.* AZ Central. Available at:
https://yourbusiness.azcentral.com/security-issues-relating-internet-banking-21683.html (Accessed: 2020).

Khatri, P. (2019) *The importance of cyber security in banking - The Global Treasurer, The Global Treasurer.* The Global Treasurer. Available at:
https://www.theglobaltreasurer.com/2019/09/25/the-importance-of-cyber-security-in-banking/ (Accessed: 2020).

Kovsky, S. (2019) *Where do CISOs Belong in an IT Org Chart?, InformationWeek.* InformationWeek. Available at:
https://www.informationweek.com/cybersecurity/where-do-cisos-belong-in-an-it-org-chart- (Accessed: March 27, 2022).

Kuppinger, M. (2019) *Redefining the role of the CISO – cybersecurity and business continuity management must become one*, *KuppingerCole*. KuppingerCole. Available at: https://www.kuppingercole.com/blog/kuppinger/redefining-the-role-of-the-ciso (Accessed: January 19, 2023).

Lewis, B. (2019) *How to Tackle Today's IT security risks*, *ISO*. International Standards Organization. Available at: https://www.iso.org/news/ref2360.html (Accessed: January 18, 2023).

McGrath, M. (2020) "Top 2020 Banking Regulations & Security Compliance Requirements," *One Span*, 1 February. Available at: https://www.onespan.com/blog/top-2020-banking-regulations-security-compliance-requirements.

Monahan, J. (2020) *Report: Critical Infrastructure Cyber Attacks A Global Crisis | The Security Ledger*, *The Security Ledger*. Security Ledger. Available at: https://securityledger.com/2020/10/report-critical-infrastructure-cyber-attacks-a-global-crisis/ (Accessed: 2021).

Muncaster , P. (2015) *Finance hit by 300 times more attacks than other industries*, *Infosecurity Magazine*. Info Security Group. Available at: https://www.infosecurity-magazine.com/news/banks-hit-300-times-more-attacks/ (Accessed: November 10, 2022).

Mutsuo, N.O.G.U.C.H.I. and Hirofumi, U.E.D.A. (2017) *An Analysis of the Actual Status of Recent Cyberattacks on Critical Infrastructures : NEC Technical Journal | NEC, NEC*. NEC. Available at: https://www.nec.com/en/global/techrep/journal/g17/n02/170204.html (Accessed: 2021).

NCES (2023) *Security Policy: Development and Implementation, Chapter 3-Security Policy: Development and implementation, from safeguarding your technology, NCES publication 98-297 (National Center for Education Statistics)*. Institute of Education Sciences. Available at: https://nces.ed.gov/pubs98/safetech/chapter3.asp (Accessed: January 16, 2023).

Near, J. and Darais, D. (2020) *Threat Models for Differential Privacy, NIST*. NIST. Available at: https://www.nist.gov/blogs/cybersecurity-insights/threat-models-differential-privacy (Accessed: 2021).

Nicodemus, A. and Nicodemus, A. (2020) *Citigroup fined $400M for compliance, risk management failures, Compliance Week*. Compliance Week. Available at: https://www.complianceweek.com/regulatory-enforcement/citigroup-fined-400m-for-compliance-risk-management-failures/29588.article (Accessed: 2020).

O'Flaherty, K. (2022) *Establishing a Strong Information Security Policy, Information Age*. Information Age. Available at: https://www.information-age.com/establishing-a-strong-information-security-policy-123500597/ (Accessed: January 5, 2023).

Petree, S. and Petree, S. (2019) *The Strategic Side of Cybersecurity Governance*, *https://www.bankdirector.com/*. Bank DIrectors.com. Available at: https://www.bankdirector.com/issues/strategic-side-cybersecurity-governance/ (Accessed: 2021).

POC to Call and interview Later is Kevin Greenfield, Deputy Comptroller for Operational Risk, at (202) 649-6550.

Pritchard , S. (2021) *The "Office of the Ciso": A new structure for cybersecurity governance*, *Tripwire*. Available at: https://www.tripwire.com/state-of-security/office-of-ciso-a-new-structure-for-cybersecurity-governance (Accessed: May 3, 2022).

Ramachandran, R. (2020) *How to become a chief information security officer (CISO)*, *Medium*. Medium. Available at: https://remeshr.medium.com/how-to-become-a-chief-information-security-officer-ciso-f6a4eeb718ff (Accessed: August 4, 2022).

Redmon, G. (2017) *Regulatory compliance: The new CISO Challenge*, *Security Intelligence*. Available at: https://securityintelligence.com/regulatory-compliance-the-new-ciso-challenge/ (Accessed: January 17, 2023).

Richter, W., Lund, F. and Noble, J. (2021) "Boards and Cybersecurity," *McKinsey&Company*, 2 February, p. 1.

Ross, P. (2022) *What is a Ciso? their role and responsibilities clearly explained: Upguard, RSS.* Available at: https://www.upguard.com/blog/what-is-a-ciso#:~:text=As%20we%20have%20seen%2C%20a,align%20with%20the%20organization%27s%20objectives (Accessed: January 21, 2023).

SANS Institute and SANS Institute (2020) *SANS Institute: Information Security Resources, Sans.org.* SANS. Available at: https://www.sans.org/information-security#:~:text=Information%20Security%20refers%20to%20the,destruction%2C%20modification%2C%20or%20disruption.* (Accessed: 2020).

Scholl, F. (2021) *Understanding root causes of trade secret breaches, CSO Online.* CSO Magazine. Available at: https://www.csoonline.com/article/3250696/understanding-root-causes-of-trade-secret-breaches.html (Accessed: 2021).

Sheltered Harbor - Home (2020) *Shelteredharbor.org.* Sheltered Harbor Organziation. Available at: https://shelteredharbor.org/ (Accessed: 2020).

Sherman & Sterling Firm (2020) *Banking Regulations 2020, GLI - Global Legal Insights.* Global Legal Insights. Available at: https://www.globallegalinsights.com/practice-

areas/banking-and-finance-laws-and-
regulations/usa#chaptercontent4 (Accessed: 2021).

Shevlin, R. (2020) "Banks' False Sense Of Cybersecurity Will
Be Shattered By Cloud Computing," *Forbes*, 1 August.

Singer, D. and Singer, D. (2020) *Five ways banks can avoid
hefty fines for poor risk management | SC Media, SC
Media*. SC Media. Available at:
https://www.scmagazine.com/perspectives/five-ways-
banks-can-avoid-hefty-fines-for-poor-risk-management/
(Accessed: 2021).

TalentLyft (2023) *Chief information security officer job
description template, Recruiting and Hiring Resources*.
TalentLyft. Available at:
https://www.talentlyft.com/en/resources/chief-
information-security-officer-job-description (Accessed:
January 16, 2023).

Townsend, K. (2021) *CISO conversations: Steve Katz, the
world's first Ciso, SecurityWeek*. Security Week.
Available at: https://www.securityweek.com/ciso-
conversations-steve-katz-worlds-first-ciso (Accessed:
February 5, 2022).

Tripwire (2023) *The changing role of the ciso, Tripwire*.
Fortra. Available at:
https://www.tripwire.com/resources/guides/the-
changing-role-of-the-
ciso#:~:text=The%20CISO%20is%20no%20longer,busi

ness%2C%20and%20to%20the%20board. (Accessed: January 17, 2023).

User, S. (2017) *ADFSL - Journal, Adfsl.org.* ADF. Available at: https://www.adfsl.org/index.php/journal (Accessed: 2021).

User, S. (2021) *ADFSL - Journal, Adfsl.org.* Available at: https://www.adfsl.org/index.php/journal (Accessed: 2021).

User, S. (2021) *ADFSL - Journal, Adfsl.org.* Available at: https://www.adfsl.org/index.php/journal (Accessed: 2021).

Vizza, T. (2023) *7 reasons why you should pursue CISSP certification, 7 Reasons Why You Should Pursue CISSP Certification.* Available at: https://www.isc2.org/Articles/7-Reasons-Why-You-Should-Pursue-CISSP-Certification (Accessed: January 21, 2023).

Wintemute, D. (2022) *How to become a CISO: Required education and experience, Explore Cybersecurity Degrees and Careers | CyberDegrees.org.* Cyber Degrees. Available at: https://www.cyberdegrees.org/careers/chief-information-security-officer-ciso/how-to-become/ (Accessed: January 11, 2023).

"OCC Bulletin 2020-5 Cybersecurity: Joint Statement on Heightened Cybersecurity Risk" (2020). Office of the Comptroller of the Currency (OCC). Available at: https://occ.gov/news-issuances/bulletins/2020/bulletin-2020-5.html (Accessed: 2020).

Annexes

Annex 1

Focus Group Participants

The participants of the first two surveys where the same 8 individuals in the Focus Group since this was based on the Delphi Methodology.

I provided a survey to a focus group made up of 8 Risk Mangers compromising both Chief Risk Officers and Enterprise Risk Managers.

Focus Group Organizations

    a) Transportation
    b) Real Estate
    c) Manufacturing/Retail
    d) Managed Service Provider
    e) Transit Infrastructure
    f) Law Firm
    g) Production (Movies)

Aviation Countries

    a) USA

Size of Organization

    a) 25

b) 30
c) 773
d) 1,750
e) 2,500
f) 11,000
g) 44,000

Titles:

- Director of Secops (security Operations)
- Chief Information Security Officer
- Director, IT Security
- Director

Annex 2

Focus Group 1

Survey for MBA in Information Security Michael C. Redmond

As part of my thesis research, I am conducting a Focus Group addressing the Role of the Chief Information Security Officer (CISO) in US Organizations. I am inviting you to be a member of the focus group. This will involve answering this questionnaire, as well as a follow-up questionnaire which will be a composite of the combined answers from the first questionnaire in order to cull the answers down to the most common results.

Thanks for accepting my invitation to be in the Focus Group and taking the time to answer this questionnaire. Please send me the response via LinkedIn Messaging as an attachment as a Microsoft Word document, not PDF, to assist me in my analysis.

Michael

Michael C. Redmond

Your identity will be kept anonymous, but for my research please put your name, title, and organization.

Your organization:

Industry:

Size of Organization:

Your Title:

Email:

Please fill in the survey questions below, adding additional space as needed.

1) What is a common definition for a Chief Information Security Officer (CISO) in an organization?

2) What is the job description for a Chief Information Security Officer (CISO) in your organization?

3) Which of these knowledge areas/experiences are critical for a Chief Information Security Officer (CISO)? Please elaborate under each.

   a) Governance, Risk and Compliance
   b) Technical knowledge and skills
   c) Managerial Experience
   d) Other

4) What Certification(s), if any, should a Chief Information Security Officer (CISO) have?

5) What responsibility should each of the following have for Cyber Security Governance? Please elaborate.

   a) Board of Directors
   b) Board of Trustees
   c) Chief Information Security Officer (CISO)
   d) Managers
   e) Employees
   f) Other

6) How has Cyber Security Governance changed in the United States in the last 5 years?

7) What are the most important aspects of Cyber Security Governance in your organization and how does this compare to other Organizations in the United States?

8) What has changed in the role of a Chief Information Security Officer (CISO) in United States Organization in the last 5 years?

9) Do you think the role of the Chief Information Security Officer (CISO) will change in the next 5 years? If yes, how?

10) What questions have I not asked that you think are important to my research on the Role of the Chief Information Security Officer (CISO)?

Annex 3

Focus Group 2

The following questions were based on the synopsis of the first survey.

The participants of the first two surveys where the same 7 individuals in the Focus Group since this was based on the Delphi Methodology.

I provided a questionnaire survey to a focus group made up of Information Security Officers

Second and Last Focus Group Survey for: MBA in Information Security Michael C. Redmond

---

October 12, 2022

Dear Survey Participant,

Thanks, so much for responding to my first survey. Please complete this survey by <u>*Saturday October21, 2022*</u>

I am using the Delphi Method of Research which includes using the same participants for culling down the response even more.

Please take a few minutes to respond to this final survey, if the results are very close. I will be happy to share my thesis with you as soon as it is published.

Below are the consolidated results. Please highlight the letter next to the paragraph under each question that you most closely agree with. You must choose one and only one.

<u>Please do not add in any comments.</u>

Thanks very much,

Michael

Michael C. Redmond

917-882-5453

Your identity will be kept anonymous in the Thesis, but for my research please put your name, title, and organization.

Name:

Your organization:

Industry:

Size of Organization:

Your Title:

Email:

The following questions includes the synopsis of the first survey.

Please highlight the letter for each question that you most closely agree with.

You must select one answer for each question. No comments should be added.

1. What is a common definition for a Chief Information Security Officer (CISO) in an organization?

   a) Responsible for defining its strategic goals as they pertain to application security, corporate security, and data governance. The CISO sets the vision for its enterprise security strategy with a clear roadmap and work closely with its leadership team across Engineering, Product, IT, and Compliance to make sure the roadmap is executed. They create, implement and maintain a security team, build on existing security policies, procedures, standards, and guidelines, and work with customers and prospects to address security concerns. Responsible for developing and implementing an information security program which entails day to day operations, which includes strategy development, operations of information and cyber security operations, budget, and project management and staffing.

   b) The Chief Information Security Officer (CISO) is the head of IT security, driving the IT security strategy and implementation forward while protecting the business from security threats and cyber-hacking. The Chief Information Security Officer is responsible for providing strategic thought leadership and measurable, defined outcomes in the oversight and delivery of a robust enterprise information security program. Key focus areas are in the establishment and direction of developing, implementing, sustaining, and enhancing enterprise information security and risk management programs Design and oversee the security related projects, as well as projects that require a security component. Keep management informed on the progress that has been made. Ensure that adequate governance is performed through the data lifecycle of firm data. Ensure that regulations are being met, keep employees and management current of the latest news that could impact the security of the firm and audit our security policies that we have developed and enacted to mitigate our security risks

c) A CISO is the role performed by a senior-level executive within an organization responsible for establishing and maintaining the infosec roadmap to protect the employees, customers and shareholders from harm. This role is sometimes fulfilled by a dual-titled CIO/CISO or CSO/CISO depending on the size and maturity of the organization. A business leader charged to build, manage, and maintain the company's security program. Responsible for implementing technical security controls and reducing cyber risk. Accountable to the Board of Directors, and charged with protecting the organization's digital assets and data, aligning security programs with business objectives, managing security, and reducing risk

d) CISO is responsible for ensuring the confidentiality, integrity and availability of an organization's information, whether it is in digital and physical format and regardless of where it is stored. A senior-level executive responsible for developing and implementing an information security program, which includes procedures and policies designed to protect enterprise communications, systems and assets from both internal and external threats. Develop enterprise-wide security programs to protect corporate systems as well such as the cloud platform for delivering security rating services to customers, executives and the boards of directors

2. Which of these knowledge areas/experiences are critical for a Chief Information Security Officer (CISO)? Please choose one under each heading.

Governance, Risk and Compliance

a) CISO drives policies and procedures to manage compliance to controls, measurement of key performance indicators, and management decisions against the data to ensure organization goals are being met. The CISO needs to assess the risks that could impact the goals of the organization, and plan, test and have contingencies for continuous operations.

Compliance to the controls is supported through aligned evidence and reporting.

b) CISO must be experienced in governance and assessing risks to properly manage a security program and make the necessary adjustments based on the business risks the company is experiencing. Without an adequate GRC program, you cannot measure the effectiveness of your programs.

c) CISO ensures that all initiatives run smoothly and receive the funding they need. Ensure corporate leadership understands their role in Cyber Security. Securing adequate resources from the board of directors, the GRC aspect of CISO work is upwards focused in the org chart. Governance is slow and items which do not persist as risk register items for more than one quarter do not qualify as board-level governance concerns. Speaking at this executive level of management and compliance, the intent is to make sure that IT controls, finance controls and security controls are integrated and tracked holistically rather than in discrete business departments/functions

Technical Knowledge and Skills

a) CISO needs technical knowledge and skills to efficiently drive the technical strategy for tools and processes and balance the costs against the risk appetite of the organization. Tools are expensive. Features, APIs, system integration, automation, etc. need to be understood to manage change, people, and process.

b) Less important, since Cyber Security Teams have Security Analysts who are technical experts to work under the CISO. They follow the policies and procedures that were approved by the CISO. The CISO needs ability to understand the technical aspects of security but not required to perform any security functions. player-coach as opposed to pure coach CISO profiles are finding their way into modern cybersecurity programs.

c) CISO is a hands-on role, with direct knowledge and participation in the tools and techniques of managing security across the organization. Real-time analysis of immediate threats, and triage.

Managerial Experience

a) Building great teams, mentoring, career, and education development, getting the most out of people while at the same time having them feel empowered and an appreciated member are skills required to be an effective CISO. Understanding skill gap, how to prioritize workloads and meeting business deadlines. Managerial experience is helpful to properly motivate his or her team in following the company's vision and mission around security.

b) Extremely important, if you cannot speak to senior management about the risks and why they need to adequately budget for security projects, then you cannot effectively perform your job. Management needs the confidence that you can supervise projects in a timely manner and within budget and communicate their benefits to management.

c) CISOs need to be influencers and they are required to wear many hats within any organization regardless of its maturity, size or industry. For this aspect of the CISO's role to be effective, they must be able to switch between different types of conversations with any of their colleagues: executive, strategic and tactical. These types of discussions include executive, strategic ,tactical, etc.

Which of these statements is most true?

a) CISO needs to be able to manage relationships with vendors and negotiate terms that are favorable to the organization. CISOs need to provide feedback and encourage the vendor to implement features when needed.

b) CISO needs to engage with other CISOs in order to receive feedback and gage the progress of its own organization. CISO needs to have a trusted community of peers to discuss challenges they face and share ideas with to grow and learn how to continuously improve their organization's security

c) CISO needs to be familiar with the various frameworks in order to map control requirements against the controls of the organization

d) CISO need to focus on resilience. Resilience is more about what happens *after* the attack and how quickly you can get back up after being hit by an attack or a breach. And it's not like the engineering definition of resilience which might have to do with tensile strength or ductile properties of metallurgy. Resilience in the cyber definition should be about adaptation, robustness and transformation after being exposed to extreme conditions and forces (such as a DDoS attack or a ransomware outbreak).

e) CISO needs to engage thoughtful experimentation regarding defense capabilities in order to take a more active posture rather than passive approach to failure. Scheduling a tabletop exercise, pentest, red team exercise or threat hunting engagement is what can be called "active defense" so a team knows who might attack, when they might attack and what techniques they are most likely to use against you. Threat intelligence and continuous monitoring are two important ingredients when bringing into existence an active defense approach.

3. What Certification(s), if any, should a Chief Information Security Officer (CISO) have?

a) CISSP as it provides a measurement of understanding for the domains covered in the certification
b) CISM
c) CCISO
d) QTE Boardroom Readiness
e) Experiences is more important than certifications. I don't believe that certifications usually equate to being qualified If they have a support staff to assist in areas

that are not their strengths, then they don't need any specific certifications.

4. What responsibility should each of the following have for Cyber Security Governance?

Board of Directors

a) Ensure that the executive team is prepared and has a plan for the eventuality of a cyber-attack. In addition, it is the boards responsibility to supporting the funding for the plan when agreed to.
b) Oversight of cybersecurity management and strategy. Ensuring that risk is understood from a legal and regulatory perspective.
c) BOD should hold the CISO and executive leadership responsible for Cyber Security. They should ask questions as needed to gain a better understanding of the Company's security posture

Board of Trustees

a) Board of Trustees are responsible to make sure that the executive team is prepared and has a plan for the eventuality of a cyber-attack
b) Oversight of cybersecurity management and strategy. Ensuring that risk is understood from a legal and regulatory perspective.
c) Should hold the CISO and executive leadership responsible for Cyber Security. They should ask

questions as needed to gain a better understanding of the Company's security posture

d) Ultimate accountability for making sure the organization has applied adequate resources to protecting the intellectual property of the business, the data of the customers and the integrity of the organization with respect to compliance and auditability for self-imposed as well as regulatory-imposed controls.

Chief Information Security Officer (CISO)

a) Responsible for the Security Program
b) Build cyber framework according to CIA triad
c) CISO is responsible for the strategy, budget and execution of the policies and procedures for Cyber Security Governance
d) Effective communication upwards, downwards and laterally within an organization.
e) CISO can be empowering a mindset of security by finding and rewarding "security champions" which are not among their direct reports. This is the area of "influence" when talking about embedding security into a company culture.

It's this mindset that is important when building and managing modern cyber security governance at the program level.

Managers

a) Responsible for supporting Cyber Security policies and the governance processes within their department.

b) Implementing the strategy, and communicating new or changing risks upwards to senior management
c) Responsible for implementing the Security Program. Managers internalize the pillars of infosec: availability, integrity and confidentiality.
d) Managers have a significant role to play in effective governance.

Employees

a) Employees are responsible for supporting policies.
b) Responsible to understanding and following the Security Program.
c) They must communicate risks.

Which is most true?

a) Contracts also play a role in cyber governance.
b) Third-party suppliers/partners must be aware of and follow established cybersecurity policies.
c) Regulatory bodies are, in many cases, not keeping up with the times. The oversight of an industry should entail strong monitoring and enforcement of breach reporting.

5. How has Cyber Security Governance changed in the United States in the last 5 years?

a) Governance has matured in the aspect of incorporating change management, vulnerability management

b) Increased focus on third-party risk management. Customers and clients have put the pressure on companies they do business with to have a formal information security program and to provide evidence like policies, MFA configurations, password policies, risk assessments, etc.

c) The board is starting to pay a closer attention to Cyber Security issues and concerns. There is a shift into greater awareness and more frequent participation of cybersecurity leadership in the overall governance functions of most companies. It is emerging from the technical weeds of IT and taking up a seat at the proverbial table

d) Regulators are starting to hold company leadership and boards responsible for security failures Boards and C-Suites recognize there is an added business risk and now seem to understand that expertise is needed at the table with the rest of the C-Suite to better understand and protected against the added risk. Leadership has taken an interest in truly defining their risk tolerance. CISOs are becoming key members of the executive leadership team.

e) Frameworks are being adopted. Policies are being implemented. Controls are being put in place, along with resiliency capabilities.

f) With more data being migrated to cloud services, there is a need for an understanding of how to govern data that is being hosted by a vendor. Cyber threats have gotten to be more severe and creative, so organization need to understand where their biggest risks are and be able to react to incidents quicker than they previously did.

6. **What is the most important aspect of Cyber Security Governance in your organization?**

a) Vulnerability Management has become priority as new hacking groups emerge and more exploits are being known the wild and what it takes to remediate these findings in the organization

b) Establishing procedures that are audit ready, ensuring logs of systems are included in our log retention system for visibility, MFA is implemented when supported, and that the culture of the organization is changing with the process changes being introduced to support governance.

c) After so many years (or decades) of being a chaotic response-only effort, the development of well-defined program aligned to a well-respected framework is the current most important aspect

d) Most important aspect of Governance is ensuring that our client's data is not compromised by an unauthorized user

e) Regular reporting to the board of directors (each quarter at a minimum) and the corporate risk register exists, is reviewed regularly, contains board-level cybersecurity governance items.

f) The average score of our core vendors/service providers is tracked as a KPI

7. **What has changed in the role of a Chief Information Security Officer (CISO) in United States Organization in the last 5 years?**

   a) CISO has become more of someone who is reporting to the board and overseeing the development of the security program. The CISO hires directors and manager in which whom takes on the responsibility to build the cyber framework and reduce risk within the organization

   b) More requirements around technology skills for CISOs. Boards are seeing the need after experiencing breaches.

   c) The biggest change has been the mindset shift of protecting the systems to protecting the 'data'. With the proliferation and adoption of third-party cloud services, the risk to the company data has significantly increased. CISOs must now communicate the risk to the data upwards. CISOs need to define and implement updated data protection controls and strategies

   d) The CISO is more of an influencer today than they were 5 years ago. The CISO must influence the board to get funding to address key concerns. The CISO must influence his team to implement his\her plan to address the key concerns

   e) The average tenure at an organization is less than 18 months for a CISO in their position with a company. There is no meaningful answer to the question "are we secure?" when asked by an executive or board member. Executive team and C-Suite do not understand that a security program is a compromise between risk appetite, cost and agreeing on an acceptable level of "residual risk" for the organization.

f) We can transfer risk with cyber insurance or outsourcing of certain capabilities or functions of the company (like purchasing a virtual SOC instead of running an in-house team to monitor security alerts and events 24x7

g) CISOs are evolving from a deeply technical role towards a more "risk management" role. Some CISOs retain that technical depth, but in addition they are adopting a more high-level approach to risk. Think perhaps of the meaning implied by evolving from simple risk management towards "risk intelligence" and taking an approach that is intent on solving problems of scale with automation and orchestration.

h) We embrace modern tools and techniques for mitigating all tiers of vendors.

8. Do you think the role of the Chief Information Security Officer (CISO) will change in the next 5 years?

a) No not in the next 5 years but in the future as our technology expands to incorporate future technology such as block chain, crypto and cloud.

b) Yes, there will be continuing change for technology skills requirements as well as CISOs leading IT

Infrastructure due to the security requirements across infrastructure and cloud.

c) Yes, the CISO role will continue evolve. With the average lifespan of a CISO role to about 2 years. A CISO needs to evolve in their role or risk being obsolete to meet the demands of the role and business requirements that are always changing and evolving.

d) Yes, CISO will have more accountability and be more compliance oriented.
They will need to be more diligent about tracking and reporting even the smallest cyber event.

e) Yes, CISO will be reporting outside of the technology org more often in the future. Instead of a CISO reporting to the CTO or CIO, they will be reporting directly to the CEO or to general counsel (Chief Risk Officer if one exists). There is often a conflict of interest when reporting security risks to the CTO/CIO who ultimately own that risk and have yet to address it, so the escalation of priorities for certain risks is muted by the current reporting structures in many organizations.

9. **What is a critical question relating to the Role of the Chief Information Security Officer (CISO)?**

a) Why when a breach occurs the CISO is the first to go? To a CISOs defense he/she is just one person who may or may not have limited staff and has got the communication to the board that in cyber there is no silver bullet.

b) Why is CISO turnover so high? Burnout?

c) What are some of the challenges to communicating upwards for CISOs (e.g. risk education)?
d) What is the path to CISO in terms of training, college major and career titles that led to the role?
e) What is the value of a CISO reaching this role by "the path less travelled" instead of a CISOs that were former computer science students/graduates?

Mitigating Corporate Risks:
an integrated view of Corporate Risk
Management

Michael C. Redmond

A Thesis in the field of Risk Management

For the degree: Master of Business Administration

PECB University
July 2020

Mitigating Corporate Risks
an integrated view of Corporate Risk Management

Michael C. Redmond, PhD   Baton Mati, PhD C.

A Thesis in the field of Risk Management

For the degree: Master of Business Administration

PECB University
July, 2020

Abstract

This thesis is a study about the most effective way to utilize Chief Risk Officers and organize the risk structure within a corporation. GE Capital created the world's first documented position of a Chief Risk Officer in 1993. Other companies followed suit. When the United States Government released Sarbanes Oxley Act in 2002 even more organizations started to implement Chief Risk Officers. In 2007 after the financial crash, the role of the Chief Risk Officer, as well as how Risk Management should be positioned within an organization was re-evaluated by many companies and studies. This thesis study examines the role, Risk Management positioning within the corporation, and if they are yet structured effectively.

The changing trends in corporations address minimizing multilevel risk. There has been a rising importance of Risk Controls due to high-profile bankruptcies (ENRON – Arthur Andersen), which is why the Sarbanes Oxley Act is/came into being. The recent crises such as the 2008 Global Financial Crisis and the Covid19 pandemic has shown how unprepared we are despite advances in the Risk Management profession.

The emphasis has changed from Risk Management just keeping an "eye" on the known financial risks and using insurance as the solution if there was an event that affected the business, to one of being proactive. It has moved to asking better questions such as what could happen to affect the business using a more quantitative and qualitative approach to risk. Questions such as what threats could affect us, where are we vulnerable, what impacts could this have on us such as loss of reputation, loss of customers, loss of market share and so many other questions.

More importantly, the emphasis includes empowering the Risk Management to make better decisions related to risk and compliance, while ensuring that proper governance is in place.

Biographical Sketch of the Author

Michael was selected for Women of Distinction Magazine in 2016 for her contribution in Information/Cyber Security field. Michael is in Who's Who among Executives and Professionals and is in the Academic and Professional National Honor Society for Continuity Planners, "Order of the Sword & Shield". She spent 4 years on Active Duty with the United States Army and 18 1/2 years in National Guard and Reserve before retiring as a Lieutenant Colonel. She is a Graduate of Command & General Staff College (Fort Leavenworth), attended Civil Affairs Courses – US Army JFK School of Special Warfare and is Hazmat Trained, DOD Certified. She has been an Adjunct Professor for University of Maryland, Mercy College, New York University and John Jay Graduate School, where she taught Business Management, Cyber/Information Security, Business Continuity, Disaster Recovery and Emergency Management. Michael was selected by the United Nations (UN) to write the prologue for the Risk Management Chapter in the UN's book on Disaster Management, which was given to the Heads of States of all member countries and, endorsed by Nelson Mandela and President Bill Clinton. She was also invited to attend a luncheon at the White House honoring her and the other attendees as the top women in their respective fields.

Acknowledgements

I'd like to extend my gratitude to PECB University for providing a supportive environment to conduct my research.

I am very grateful to Baton Mati, Director of Academic Affairs for all the countless hours serving as my Thesis Advisor.

Special thanks to Ivana Stevanovic, PECB University School Librarian, for her guidance in my research.

I wish to pay special regards to my daughter Brie C. Pfisterer, for listening and providing objective feedback when I was developing my Thesis Proposal.

It is with great appreciation, that I thank the professionals who took part in my focus groups and provided invaluable qualitative data.

Student Declaration

5. I declare that this dissertation is my original work. I further certify that no parts of it, nor its entirety has been previously submitted for a degree, diploma or certificate in any university or other academic/certification body. This dissertation has not been copied from other published materials; be it other students' theses or based on any other source except those sources that have been cited appropriately throughout this document, or for which there exists an explicit description in the text.

6. I hereby grant permission to PECB University and PECB University Library to lend or copy this dissertation for digital storage, inclusion of the same in the thesis section of the library and make it available for academic and research purposes.

7. I have read and understood, and also adhere to all stipulations made in PECB University's Academic Dishonesty Policy; as such, I declare that to the best of my knowledge I have not committed any action that can be described as a dishonest practice within the frameworks of this policy.

8. All views and conclusions stated herein represent my views as the author, and they may not necessarily represent the positions or views of PECB University and/or its Faculty.

Dr. Michael C Redmond, PhD

Author   Date & Signature

Michael C. Redmond   _____

Abbreviations

CEO- Chief Executive Officer

CFO- Chief Financial Officer

COSO- Committee of Sponsoring Organizations of the Treadway Commission

COVID 19- Coronavirus 2019

CRO - Chief Risk Officer

ERM - Enterprise Risk Management

GE-General Electric

IARCP- International Association of Risk and Compliance Professionals

ISACA - Information Systems Audit and Control Association

ISO-International Standards Organization (ISO)

OCTAVE- Operationally Critical Threat, Asset, and Vulnerability Evaluation

NIST- National Institute of Standards and Technology (NIST) Risk Management Framework.

PWC -Price Waterhouse Coopers

Introduction

The research that focuses on utilizing Risk Management towards making major business decisions has witnessed a considerable amount of debate in the recent years – alas in a limited areas of industries and operations. On the other hand, a thorough examination of the underlying issues regarding business decision-making without utilizing Risk Management lacks proper attention by scholars. Hence, many organizations limit the use of Risk Management to common areas such as Information Technology, Information Security, production / manufacturing, insurance, and finance.

Every aspect of the business including fields such as marketing and human resources among others, should follow the risk process. Risk Managers' job scope needs to be enhanced to include the entire business operations. Categorizing risk by business strategy risk, compliance risk, operational risk, financial risk and reputational risk are not claimed to be enough if they are only applied to certain high-level areas of the organization.

According to an article written two decades ago in National Underwriter, a Risk Manger must keep their skills up by challenging themselves to expand the areas of risk in a corporation that needs to follow a risk process (Pouzar, 1993). This includes marketing, production, international business opportunities, and all of the key business functions that are part of an organization.

Even 27 years after the article by National Underwriter, this research is showing that although the processes may have improved, the programs have not. According to an article by A. Levin (1997), a market survey conducted by Price Waterhouse Coopers clearly indicated that risk managers need to expand their scope of activities, A recommendation that will be further examined in this paper is if risk managers have done so and has it expanded to meet the risks.

In another approach to this topic Peter Pelzer wrote in Society and Business Review that the methods used in Risk Management can only be used by risk managers and can be intimidating to those who are not. (Pelzer, P. 2009)

Even in today's world, the perception of Risk Management and the proper use of Risk Mangers in organizations is a topic that has not been studied well enough – meaning that the roles are not clear; the RMs are not utilized efficiently and risks go unattended. Hence, in light of the recent events on a global stage that have tested the Risk Management scope to the limit, this paper will seek to re-examine the role of Risk Managers within an organization

Focus of the Discussion

History has many examples of organizations, or rather the people in the organizations, who have made poor decisions. The impacts of these poor decisions have had different results, but the consequences for some have been devastating.

There is enough evidence from the real world to atone for the importance of Risk Management and their involvement throughout all organizational activities; such as a historical analysis on the purchase of Louisiana, and the controversial launching of a new Coke product that failed drastically in the market.

Looking at risk from governing countries as a point of view, in 1803, the purchase of Louisiana from France turned out to be a good decision: it had doubled the size of the United States by 100% and helped with farmers' loyalty. It also helped to circumvent a potential war with France. But from a risk point of view, it meant spending a lot of money for a country that did not have much. It was a necessary course of action; Napoleon Bonaparte needed the money for the Great French War and he was involved with the Haitian Revolution, he could not at the time defend Louisiana against Britain. (Milestones: 1801–1829 - Office of the Historian, 2020)

Switching the perspective from governing countries to managing organizations, an interesting case could be made when Excite passed on purchasing Google for $750,000 in 1999 because the CEO felt there was too much of a cultural difference since Google wanted its search engine used and Excite felt it would pull people away from their site. (McCullough, 2014) From research it appears a formal risk assessment was not done, and Risk Managers were not consulted.

Another interesting high-profile situation of failing to adhere to proper Risk Management principles is when in 1985 Coca-Cola put New Coke on the market not considering the risk of ignoring the pop culture of the time. This proved a fatal error for the New Coke Product. When the company conducted taste tests, they failed to ask if customers wanted it. Customers in the US Southwest were so upset by the change to a staple product, that the company hired a psychiatrist to listen in on complaint calls. After only 79 days the new coke product was removed from the market. (Haasch, 2019) If Risk Managers were involved in Marketing and New Product Development, these scenarios would probably have been foreseen and averted.

Ross Perot passing on an offer to purchase stakes at Microsoft in 1979 is also a well-known story. He felt the price was too high and said in an interview that he should have asked Gates what he felt was fair. (Al-Thani and Merna, 2008) The decision was based on present use for the company, not about the risk of not moving into a micro based market. In retrospective, a Risk Manager would have considered moving market trends and the ability to proliferate the market (Al-Thani and Merna, 2008).

Building on these cases, and looking to define Risk Management, Robert Half a well-known placement firm in the field, has a Risk Manger job description that limits the duties to those affecting the financial impact of the company. It essentially outlines that such a position is responsible to create a Risk Management process that includes financial analysis if an adverse event occurs. It does not mention the qualitative analysis that should take as part of the risk process. (Robert Half, 2019)

Contrastingly, ISO.org when referencing ISO 31000:2018 Risk Management Guidelines states, "Risks affecting organizations can have consequences in terms of economic performance and professional reputation, as well as environmental, safety and societal outcomes. Therefore, managing risk effectively helps organizations to perform well in an environment full of uncertainty." ("ISO 31000 Risk management", 2019) This international standard can be applied to all areas of a business.

Problem Definition

Companies experience events that they later reflect in hindsight could have been mitigated if they had recognized the risks. The problem for such organizations relates to why were the risks not identified and mitigated earlier. In this sense, this paper seeks to identify if Risk Managers are being used properly and if the Risk Managers are involved throughout the enterprise.

Study objectives and relevance

The defined problem is, that companies experience events that they later reflect, in hindsight, could have been mitigated if they had recognized the risks.

All this is relevant because it will enable a better way to organize Risk Management within a corporation and to create better risk cultures in order to mitigate threats that affect corporations.

Literature Review

Reorganization of Risk Management

In the early 1990's many corporate crises occurred, making the role of a corporate Risk Manager or CRO seem the natural solution. The CRO's presence gave others the sense they could take riskier chances or not want to miss out on business opportunities. (Aebi, Sabato and Schmid, 2012)

This false sense of security was accompanied by a feeling that Risk Management was the responsibility of the CRO and that individuals within the corporation were not responsible for handling and leveraging risk. According to a research article by Pernell, Jung and Dobbin this is referred to by Psychologists as "*moral licensing effect*" (2017, 2019). Executives felt that since there was a CRO who was responsible and supervising the organization, they did not have to police their own irresponsible decisions.

After the 2007 financial crisis, a study which surveyed 300 CFO's was sponsored by Deutsche Bank Securities, Inc. and the Global Association of Risk Professionals (GARP). The authors of the study, Henri Servaes, Ane Tarmayo and Peter Tufane, found that Risk Management needed to be part of the strategies and also objectives needed to be better defined whereas a new culture of Risk Management needed to emit throughout the organization (Servaes, Tamayo and Tufano,

2009), to balance the moral licensing that organization's staff afford themselves.

Line managers should be taking risks into consideration when planning their processes and strategies. Even the risk function objectives should be subject to evaluation. Moreover, it is essential to have a risk culture throughout the origination, where each and every employee embraces Risk Management daily. Threats are always changing and organizations need to change to be able to keep up.

An eighteen-month research study focusing on risk culture was funded by the Economic and Social Research Council (ESRC), The Chartered Insurance Institute (CII), The Chartered Institute of Management Accountants (CIMA), The Lighthill Risk Network, London School of Economics and Political Science as well as Plymouth University. The findings were that risk culture is continuously changing in organizations. Also, it was observed that there may be numerous cultures within one organization. Executives find it difficult to clearly define their risk cultures within the business units and clearly delineating which areas of the business have a good risk knowledge. This awareness incongruence poses a challenge for many originations. (Power, Ashby and Palermo, 2012.)

Governance is essential as part of managing risks. A prime example of a situation where proper risk governance was missing is Wells Fargo. Not only were internal controls missing that would have caught the actions of employees who were opening accounts without permission of customers, but employees also felt the need to make their goals at any cost, even resorting to cheating (Tayon, 2019). Another example is Exxon Mobil Corporation. They were prone to a disaster that occurred in March 1989 when a tanker, owned by Exxon Mobil had a collision with a reef, and 11 million gallons of crude oil spilled into Alaska's Prince William Sound killing wildlife. Not only did they have poor governance in the Exxon Mobil disaster, but their investors even questioned their risk governance related to climate change (Lubber, 2019).

The lack of good practices related to Risk Management, including effective risk assessments and controls leads to undue risk being undertaken. Boards and Executives may be following hunches instead of looking at Risk Management practices (Hodge, 2019); furthermore, board members may also no longer be qualified to understand the modern risks that organizations are facing such as new cyber events, new environmental concerns and even new markets that are opening in areas that they are not familiar with. Risk Management needs to be more a part of organizations practices to allow them to be ready to face change and premediate negative impacts.

In search for the Perfect Risk Organization

Michael Berman, when writing about CRO's in the past, spoke about their impact regarding risk management. Since management generally perceived that their responsibility was to make profits, most of their efforts were spent in this direction, rather than reducing risks that might affect operations in the future. With this as their priority and focus, CRO's were not supported by the organization, and hence risks were not effectively managed (Berman, 2019). Ultimately, when a CROs in an organization is not supported, they have less impact to managing the risks and adding controls. This can result in many impacts including quantitative and qualitative, and also affect the organizations stock prices.

The human factor takes into consideration, errors in production, waning customer interests, political situations that can affect business operations, and more. Risk involves so much more than just financial and insurance calculations. When analyzing data about risks, it is important to remember that the risk ratings are also based on human behavior as a factor in vulnerabilities.

Beck found that those concerned with finance were experimenting with society as engineers do in a lab (Boyd, Beck and Shrader-Frechette, 1993). They were simply looking at financial impacts and ignoring the many vulnerabilities that can have an impact on risk. They Contemporary Data Engineers and Data Scientists came to understand that the human interaction with data is as important as the data itself.

Organizations such as corporations, firms, government agencies, military and other organizations are operating in an unstable environment which can lead to a number of different crisis situations. The world in which corporations operate is constantly changing and new threats are developing causing organizations to identify vulnerabilities not previously considered. The approach to Risk Management infers development and adaption at the same rate - in order to protect an organization and its assets. (Carrel, 2010.)

Meyer and Ujah, in their paper about managed earnings, found the major units of business are operations, finance and marketing (Meyer and Ujah, 2017). Specifically, companies have a tendency to distinguish between operation, market and financial risks. Not only do they measure them differently, but they also do not correlate the risks and subsequent findings. Each is treated in isolation and they also ignore risks that are not in their own specific categories. As the world evolves, so do the risks that must be considered. The correlation between different functions of an origination as well as the categories of risk considered, cannot be silted if a company wants to have true risk management (Stulz, 2019).

On this subject, although their study was limited to only Japanese and Korean companies, Shimuizu along with his colleagues, Park and Choi found that Risk Management is an operational and strategic criticality. Customer expectations are changing and so is the competitive environment (Shimizu, Park & Choi, 2014). Three years later Meidell and Kaarbøe (2017) validated the same statement in their research as being still true. The changing customer expectations, as well as organizational change that requires risk controls can affect risk management.

Lisa Meulbroek describes risk integration well, "integration refers both to the aggregation of all risks faced by the firm into a net exposure and to the coordinated use" (Meulbroek, 2002). This relates to building the perfect risk organization. Integrating risk management throughout the organizations creates a culture whereby risk is a primary concern, and not an afterthought. Having well trained Risk Managers that work with the entire organization incorporates a more holistic approach to mitigating and treating risks.

Risk Management Governance and Board Supervision

As covered previously, the discipline of Risk Management is no longer just concerned with financial risk, and there is an increasing awareness regarding the need for Risk Management in organizations. Stakeholder fears are ever increasing (Woods, 2011). Among those, Board Members and Executives must consider all of the stakeholders who fear that any risks are not identified which may have drastic results; employees who are not trained on identifying vulnerabilities or even the threats that may affect their areas; as well as potential customer concerns.

As corporate governance related to Risk Management has improved, there has been more pressure for a holistic approach that would include both financial and non-financial risks (Ariz, Manab and Othman, 2015). There should be full support from the top management for Strategic Risk Management – an organizational field that deals with the business strategy and is the process of identifying, analyzing, managing the associated risks; to ensure that it is fully incorporated into organizational business plans as well as prioritization of the associated risks (The National Law Review, 2019). Most scandals related to corporations and catastrophes related to the environments and other areas have been a result of poor Risk Management within corporate governance (Ariz, Manab and Othman, 2015).

Successful organizations are often associated with good Risk Management practices. Proper Governance of Risk Management by Boards, Executives and Managers, in organizations includes annual if not more frequent reviews of risk management, including results of audits and addressing new threats that may be occurring. Governance includes outlining and determining responsibilities as well as accountability. Allocating adequate resources is just as essential - as part of installing good governance in organizations.

Growing popularity of the Enterprise Risk Management

Corporate Risk Management originally stared as part of financial risk planning and controls, and later expanded into what we know as Risk Management and insurance risk. When Enterprise Risk Management (ERM) came into play, new techniques to quantify and qualify risks were embraced, with the likes of decision tree analysis, statistical sampling, critical chain, and PERT (program evaluation and review technique) coming into the spotlight. Yet silos still exist both in research and in practice (McShane, 2018).

In the early stages, ERM was used to describe the area of Risk Management dealing with keeping the business in operation in a situation where operations were impacted such as: Business Continuity, Disaster Recovery, Emergency Management,

Information Security, Cyber Security and more. Power referred to the study by Boyd, Beck and Shrader-Frechette from 1993, as symptomatic instead of planning for the future (Power,2019). Symptomatic involves dealing with the known threats and planning includes planning for the worst-case scenario.

Early on, Enterprise Risk Management was not the responsibility of the Chief Risk Management Officer. For more, the interconnectedness of risks between ERM and the other domains were not considered (Power, 2009). To make matters worse, the governance capabilities of boards and executive management were often lacking (Snyder, 2019).

Organizations who embraced ERM have shown promising results in handling unforeseen changes. A prime example are the organizations that were fully prepared to respond to continuing operations when COVID 19 first occurred.

Establishing True Enterprise Risk Management in Organizations

Committee of Sponsoring Organizations of the Treadway Commission (COSO) defines ERM as *"the culture, capabilities and practices, integrated with strategy-setting and performance that organizations rely on to manage risk in creating, preserving and realizing value"*. (PWC, 2016)

For example, Gatzert and Schmit speak about ERM to manage reputation risks of the entire organization and how it supports the strategies of the organizations that need to manage opportunities. A good reputation can help an organization bring in greater results or it can be lost in an instant through an action that is not the fault of the organization as a whole. (Gatzert and Schmit, 2016). A hypothetical case where a reputation can be affected by an advertisement, is when it does not consider risks such as having a well-known spokesperson who has ties with a political party which is not well received by 50% of the customers' base. Other examples of reputation taking a hit from lack of risk controls is when an organization is not able to meet product demand due a vendor not being available; an occurrence of a breach of customer data, a top executive being arrested, among others.

Companies must have common methodologies, common policies, and common processes to approach risk from an enterprise wide level (McCafferty, 2016). Case studies on Mitchell Industries, Eli Lilly and Daisy Company conducted in 2016, found that from 2009 to 2016 these companies took steps to align strategic planning and Enterprise Risk Management (ERM) ensuring a better inclusion of ERM into the strategic planning and aligning it with business strategies for the organization on a holistic level (Do, Railwaywalla and Thayer, 2016).

Organizations can choose which Risk Management Framework they wish to follow when considering enterprise risks. Some examples of Risk Management Frameworks are Operationally Critical Threat, Asset, and Vulnerability Evaluation (OCTAVE), the Committee of Sponsoring Organizations of the Treadway Commission (COSO) Risk Management Framework, International Standards Organization (ISO) specifically the ISO 31000 which covers Risk Management, National Institute of Standards and Technology (NIST) Risk Management Framework, MassMutual Pinwheel framework. Finding one that aligns with the culture and business processes is key.

Establishing ERM in organization helps organizations to better considering threats and vulnerabilities and to better control risks across the organization. When aligned with the business strategies it is easier to implement, and future-proofs the organization when it comes to Risk planning and controls.

Enterprise Risk Management today

Enterprise Risk Management (ERM) is now an established management practice and is increasing in prominence as more firms spend substantial resources implementing ERM frameworks, partially induced by regulatory requirements. Drawing on survey data from 260 of the largest firms in Denmark, Sax and Anderson (2018) found that integrating ERM with strategic planning is associated with higher profitability.

While for some organizations, Risk Management is only implemented because they are required to, other organizations understand that integrating Risk Management into the business helps control risks. Practitioners now understand that risk management includes many types of risks including, but not limited to intangible, financial, global and strategic risk (Green, 2015). On that note, Kaplan and Mikes research determined that

Risk Management is often implemented simply as a compliance requirement (Kaplan & Mikes, 2012), another paper from University of Brescia in Italy found that a Risk Management approach must be integrated (Gennari, Gandini and Cassano, 2014). While being compliant with requirements helps, it does work better when the controls are fully implemented into the business practices and a culture of managing risks prevails throughout the organization.

In order to ensure full integration throughout the organization, Risk Management as a function should report directly to Senior Management and not be under the control of any business line. There has been scholarly support to the claim that The Chief Risk Officer should have access to the Board as needed (International Finance Corporation, 2012).

Even today many organizations incorporating risk management throughout the enterprise, and risks are being considered in silos instead of across the organization. The role of the Chief Risk Officer (CRO) has expanded, yet some are simply reviewing risks associated with new projects and not revisiting risk assessments to include new threats for the entire organization.

Risk Management in the Organizational Structure

The Chief Risk Officer must include ERM among the areas for which they are responsible for as well as other corporate risk areas. This is important to ensure that the Risk Management findings are being shared across the organization. (Erm.ncsu.edu, 2019)

As defined, *"the Risk Management function is responsible for identifying, measuring, monitoring, controlling or mitigating, and reporting on risk exposures."* International Association of Risk and Compliance Professionals (IARCP). As an extension to the guidelines of International Finance Corporation (2012), research has confirmed that many CROs report directly to the Chief Executive Officer (CEO) and have direct relationship with the board (Stein, 2016).

Integrating Risk Management into the business culture is becoming a more common practice throughout organizations, and also Risk Management is more readily utilized and incorporated in organizational projects as well as aligned with overall business strategies. It goes without saying that RM must be a natural part of all areas of the business (Hillson, 2019).

To be effective, Risk Management needs oversight by a good governance program and effective risk controls, as well as independent reviews (Na.theiia.org, 2013). Furthermore, a process should be in place for the different levels to communicate and share knowledge (Al-Thani and Merna, 2013). Communication and knowledge sharing helps the risk analysis process across the organization, allowing for a better Enterprise Risk Management program.

Risk Accountability

In the past, risk committees driven by Risk Management departments would report exposure and risks to an executive risk committee who might enforce rules to maintain risks within the desired boundaries. The notion of accountability is essential to creating a culture that is to go far beyond the notions of practice, code of conduct or even a discipline of risk management. (Carrel, 2010)

A study done by Hazssan and Yawer (2013) in Pakistan found that a strong Risk Management program gave a corporation a competitive advantage. There are many examples where a strong Risk Management program would have been a help in keeping a company in business. For instance, Kodak failing to conduct thorough Risk Management practices on changing trends and competitive advantage, was surprised to find out that they were falling behind in digital imaging market and may not be able to catch up. On another industry, BlackBerry failed to consider the risk of not competing with Apple's iPhone on features that its flagship devices did not possess (Hodge, 2019). This led to them being acquired in 2013 by TCL, a Chinese consumer-electronic company who bought the phone brand (Appolonia, 2019). Apple on the other hand, is thriving as a multinational technology company.

Revisiting Risks in 2020

Threats and risks change over time. 'Executive Perspectives on Top Risks for 2020' report by Poole College North Carolina

State of Management, survey respondents were asked to rate 30 different risks involving macroeconomic, strategic, and operational issues. The top 10 risks identified were: regulatory changes, economic conditions, ability to retain top executives, legacy IT infrastructure, resistance to change , cyber threats, privacy/identity management, timely identification of risk issues, customer demographic shifts, digital technologies up-skill and re-skill" (Poole College North Carolina State of Management, 2019).

Price Waterhouse Coopers (PWC) conducted a survey in October 2019 with 3,501 CEO's in 83 territories and determined that top threats as considered by executives - differed by region. In North America the top perceived threats were cyber threats and policy uncertainty, in Asia-Pacific top threats related to trade conflicts and uncertain economic growth, in Western Europe threats preside over regulation and trade conflicts, in CEE threats relate to the availability of key skills and geopolitical uncertainty, in Middle East also geopolitical uncertainty and cyber treats are considered top threats, in Latin America populism and over-regulation, and in Africa top threats as considered by surveyed executives include policy uncertainty and availability of key skills (PWC, 2019). A common denominator on a global scale relates to international corporations, where regional threats take precedence, the likes of natural disasters known to a geographic region, or threats of local unrests or wars.

A quote by Standard Bank's CEO, Africa's Biggest Lender by Assets, is a great reminder of risk management, "My predecessors would have made a lot of decisions based on their experience and intuition. They are still very important, but you have got to triangulate them with data. As I always say: "In God we trust; everybody else, bring data." (PWC, 2019).

The importance of taking environment/economic/health threats as a top risk cannot be overstated. In 2020 Covid19 brought a worldwide threat into fruition. With it came new correlated risks and business continuity measures. People were working from home, customers could only access products online because stores were closed on governmental orders, restaurants could only deliver to homes using contactless delivery, there were shortages on some supplies, factories were closed, and more. The organizations that had not considered the threat of a Pandemic and had not planned for such events in their Enterprise Risk Management plans – along with the associated risks, were greatly surprised and unprepared. The economical results of these actions are yet to be seen.

Conclusion of Literature Review

The perception of Corporate Risk Management as a prime topic of this thesis has changed over time since the 90's as corporations have matured. Risks are much more decentralized than they have been in previous decades, mainly as a result of globalization and new treads in technology, meaning that a holistic approach is warranted.

The role of a Risk Manager has developed from 1993 when GE Capital hired James Lam as the first Chief Risk Officer, who was predominately concerned with derivatives. The 2007 financial crisis resulted in a study by Deutsche Bank Securities, Inc. and the Global Association of Risk Professionals which only surveyed CFO's about their views of Risk Management. This study was references by many studies since, ignoring the fact that those interviewed were predominately infested in derivatives and financial products, not the threats to the organization as a whole.

Risk culture is continuously changing in organizations, and executives find it challenging to define their risk cultures. A false belief is that business units can define their threats and determine the risks, while having a Chief Risk Officer that reviews reports. Risk management as a function should report directly to Senior Management and not be under the control of any business line.

The business units are not trained in risk management, and as events have shown there are corporations who have experienced adverse results related to financial aspects, public relations, regulatory issues and many other undesirable occurrences that stem from poor risk management. Enterprise Risk Management from a Marco level has been expanded to include the risks that the corporation may incur. Two decades ago, Enterprise Risk Management was predominately concerned with risks that could affect the operations of corporations while concentrating on risk disciplines such as Business Continuity Management, Information Security, Emergency Management or Physical and Logical Security.

Enterprise Risk Management has been transformed and redefined to include all areas of business risk including finance, indemnity, operations, and strategy. Corporations today are exposed to many day to day risks including legal, operational, financial, human, and many more, hence the need for ERM and dedicated CRM in organizations.

Boards and Executives are starting take more responsibility for governing risk and setting guidelines based on ethics and good business, but as business environment changes, so should the organizations and ensuing responsibility to handle change and risk that comes from it.

Research Questions

Following the extensive literature review, it became obvious that there is a general confusion when it comes to defining the roles of Risk Managers across industries. From what it became apparent from previous research, organizations conduct business decision-making without utilizing Risk Management and limiting the use of Risk Management to common areas such as Information Technology, Information Security, production / manufacturing, insurance, and finance, while ignoring other areas of the organization that present risks.

This thesis resulted in the following research questions that would lead to a better understanding of mitigating risk and integrating corporate risk management:

1. What can Risk Managers do themselves to be better utilized?
2. Why are Risk Managers reviewing the risk of the work done by others who are not specialized or trained in this area, instead of actually helping in the risk and impact analysis up front?
3. Instead of management telling business units to consider risks, why don't they require a Risk Manager conduct risk assessment for all new projects that can have negative impacts to the business?

Answering these questions would help in understanding if Risk Managers are being used properly or if there is more that they can accomplish in managing risks within the organization.

Research Methodology

Research Strategy

Planning for the research strategy for this paper is highly related to cross-referencing the already established connotations of the current extent of Risk Managers' responsibilities, with the actual (and changing) practices of the RM profession in real life. The research approach included researching the premise and various scenarios that may provide different interpretation or insight over the defined problem. Specifically, due to the nature of the research question, when it comes to the primary research, a qualitative approach fitted the thesis naturally, especially using Focus Groups as a targeted population sample.

The main goal of the research process was to provide objective insights about the scope of the Risk Manager profession, which would result in a relatively agreed upon definition – as a result of merging theory and practice on this topic.

To get the objective results from a quantitative study, the research was conducted in two sets of open-end question surveys using the Delphi Method. The Delphi Method "is a process framework based on the results of multiple rounds of questionnaires sent to a panel of experts." (Twin, 2020) This entailed different rounds of questionnaires being sent to a focus group of experts made up of Risk Managers who have over 10 years' experience in the field. The focus group members were from the United States, Australia, and Canada. I based the country sampling on the research following Hofstede's Cultural Dimensions Theory which delienates country-specific vaules that relate to behavior, including here risk handling (the uncertainty avoidance dimension). (Hofstede, 1984) Apart from their similartiy when it comes to Uncertainty Avoidance, these countries were chosen because all of these economic systems share similar organizational culture, values and systems; and all of them are derivatives of highly industrialized economies, which have been utilizing risk management methodologies for over two decades, and are well involved in international business – meaning more experience with both risk exposure and risk management. (Goncalves and Xia, 2015)

A questionnaire survey was developed and distributed to the focus group via email. The responses were then compiled and analyzed. The research strategy was to analyze using a qualitative approach. The results were then shared with the focus group panel of experts after the first questionnaire survey set was conducted by including them in the next questionnaire survey. The results were then culled down even further for commonality by including them in the creation of the next questionnaire survey which was given to the same focus group. The responses were again analyzed systematically in the same fashion to the first time, and the final results for the focus group were determined.

To add another perspective to the research problem, a separate questionaire survey was conducted which was comprised of questions based on the final results of the focus group questionnaire survey. This survey's population was diverse and targeted – the respondents were top tier managers and auditors who as employees, interact with the Risk Manager as part of their role.

The respondents for this second questionnaire were from North America, Asia, Middle East and Europe. While the United States, Canada and Australia adopted Risk Managment Practices early on, this thesis wanted to check how organizations from a more global perspective are dealing with RM issues, since in recent years the premise of risk handling has witnessed considerable changes. This is why Asia, the Middle East and Europe were included in this second questionaire survey.

Research Analysis

The analysis was conducted utilizing qualitative methods.

I conducted the focus-group survey twice I succession using the Delphi Method using a group comprised of international risk managers from a varied group of industries. I chose the Delphi Method because of the accuracy of the results collected from structured groups as opposed to unstructured groups.

The initial Focus Group 'interview sheet' included open end questions and answers. All of the focus group participants gave their own opinion without being bound/biased by multiple choices or knowing the other focus group members' opinions. By utilizing open end questions, I was able to elicit relevant information without limiting their answers.

In the second round with the Focus Group I aggregated their replies in 3 multiple choice questions and asked them to find a majority opinion. The questions were prepared by extrapolating the resulting answers that the majority of respondents agreed upon in the initial Focus Group 'interview sheet', and incorporating them into the multiple-choice questions.

To recapitalize, after the first round, the answers were analyzed and grouped by similarity into a summarizing response – which were then written down as multiple-choice options for the same questions asked in the initial survey

The first time I sent the Focus Group questionnaire survey 'interview sheet' with open ended answers, where all focus group participants gave their own opinion without being bound/biased by multiple choices or knowing other focus group members' opinions. After the first round the answers were analyzed and grouped by similarity into a summarizing response – which were then written down as multiple-choice options for the same questions that were asked in the initial survey. These were resent as a second Focus Group survey to the same participants to have them review the answers and either confirm or change their response from the first survey after rereading the response. This enabled the convergence to the answer that most closely represented the weighted opinions of all focus group participants.

For the second part of the research, I then targeted top tier business managers and auditors who are employees of organizations from around the world with a survey based on the results of the focus group survey. This led to a better benchmarking of the focus-group survey findings who shared the inside perspective of Risk Management, with other managers in organizations who shared their opinion as non-professionals in the field.As a result of one of the bigger crises that the world is currently facing, this survey also had questions related to pandemic preparations (especially relevant for the Covid19 crisis) by Risk Managers and their interaction with their Board since this was a risk that affected most organizations during the time of the survey.

Data Collection

For the research part of the thesis, the data was collected from two sources: it was collected via email for a Focus Group that participated in the in-depth survey conducted through the Delphi method; and it was collected via LinkedIn private messages for a targeted mass survey of relevant professionals who participated in the follow-up survey. The Focus Group was composed of selected professionals from LinkedIn and recommendations of professionals that should be included.

Regarding the secondary research, I referenced materials included in current periodicals and business publications, as well as textbooks and well-established periodicals. This allowed me to review current views as well as past views. Through using business, government and educational research materials I was able to ascertain a broader knowledge base.

Nature of Data

Data collected was qualitative and was derived from both primary and secondary sources. I utilized secondary sources including existing research and studies, articles, periodicals, books and journals by using data generated from desktop research. All the primary data research was conducted expressly for the purposes of this thesis.

Data Reliability and Relevance

In order to ensure that the focus-group data is as reliable as possible, I repeated the survey twice using the Delphi method, and that in two different survey formats: one being an open-end answer-seeking questionnaire, and the other being a multiple choice (based on the results of the open-end survey) in order to check whether there were answer variations from the participants for the same questions.

The reliability of the secondary data is based on the peer-published articles found through academic databases such as ProQuest, as well as publishing houses that cover books etc.

Whereas considerable effort has gone into this research, especially towards impartiality and objectivity, there is always the case that having a larger sample size may add value to this research and provide further arguments to the changing concepts of the roles of Risk Managers in today's world.

This research and the data that I have used and generated is relevant for the academia and the risk management profession.

It shows only the development in Risk Management but also where weaknesses in the use of Risk Managers still exists in some organizations and how they can be used more effectively.

Research Limitations

A quantitative analysis was done using two focus groups since it is impossible to survey the entire population because of cost, time and practicality. One focus group of Risk Managers for the first part of the research, and a more diverse group of top tier managers and auditors for the second part of the research. There is limited research in this field and many of the articles and periodicals were written prior to the last ten years. The last decade has experienced many international and technological changes that affect business risk that affect Risk Managers and there has been little coverage of the effect.

This thesis is based on the opinions of many professional from diverse organizations and country affiliations. The research shows that their practice of Risk Management has been moving in the wrong direction and many organizations are limiting risk managers responsibilities to financial, business continuity, and cyber security risks. They are not expanding their responsibilities to include intangible risks associated with poor quality control, marketing and public relations risks from the customers' perspective; instead they focus only on the legal ramifications, and other needed areas. This impedes and limits the outreach of this and similar research because although Risk Managers understand how they can and should be better utilized, the organizations do not.

Research Results

Corporations are facing more risks today than in the past because of globalization, the growing number of regulations, ever developing technology, increased competition from around the world, difficulties for small corporations to maintain corporate pricing vs. profits, and the proliferation of newly developed threats.

The study undertaken in this paper will help organizations to reevaluate their risk management practices, the role of Chief Risk Officers, training business units in risk evaluation and provide them the tools to assist building Risk Management instead of simply assigning it to them as a responsibility. The objective is to reach a better understanding of the scope of Risk Management and Risk Governance methods in organizations.

Research Part 1: the Focus Group

The first questionaire survey distributed to the focus group was the open-end answer survey. Respondents were asked to provide their insights on their (perceived) roles in the organization and more. From the survey data, it was found out that in 62 - 75 percent of organizations, Risk Managers are fully utilized in Operations and in the Information/Cyber Security departments/units. Whereas, for the areas of Marketing, Business Continuity, Disaster Recovery, Business Strategy and International Business only 50 percent or less of the originations utilize a Risk Manager.

When asked about the role and duties that affect the authority of Risk Managers, in almost 40 percent of organizations, when an individual is appointed as a Risk Manager, the reach of such position's authority tends to be very large, because most organizations are falling behind in their compliance obligations due to the ever-increasing number of laws that must be followed and considered. The survey respondents agree that the Risk Officer is an interdepartmental business enabler, problem solver and an asset in times of uncertainty, who work with process owners and managers to mitigate risk. The survey findings furthermore suggest that process owners are mainly responsible for implementation, whereas the Risk Officer establishes the oversight, control and discipline to drive continuous improvement of an organization's Risk Management capabilities in a constantly changing operating environment. They are seen as being responsible for knowing the system and the processes and understanding the risks associated with evaluating and planning Risk Management to ensure consistency and accuracy of practice; as well as facilitating and driving organization's risk management capabilities.

Conversely, per focus group respondents, in almost 40 percent of organizations there is no specific Risk Management in place. Respondents claim that the lack of Risk Managers relates to the inexistence of legislative requirements in their industry to manage risks and conduct audits. Furthermore, some respondents even claimed that their organizations are rather focused on financial and compliance risks rather than having an organization-wide Enterprise Risk Management.

Research findings also suggest that there are no legislative requirements in most industries to enterprise risks and conduct audits. In these industries, legislation that requires Risk Management committees, does not mention information security and data protection as well as other enterprise risk areas as a requirement for consideration. There is no definition or job description for Risk Managers in some companies.

In many organizations all managers and all staff are expected to actively participate in the management of risk. They actively identify, communicate and respond to expected, emerging or changing risks; contribute to the process of developing Risk Management plans for their area; and implement and monitor risk plans within their area of responsibility. A Risk Manager is trained in the process and in developing plans unlike the managers and staff.

Research part 2: The Mass Survey

Following the findings from the Focus Group research, the second part of the research comprised of a multiple-choice survey that was filled by 68 Top Tier Managers and Auditors worldwide.

From them, approximately 62 to 70 percent at least somewhat believe that Risk Managers utilized throughout their organization are formally trained and specialized and/or received their training from work or experience. Almost 30%

believe that their Risk Managers have no formal training or no training at all.

The Risk Mangers only review the Risk Assessments done by Project Managers, Functional and Business area and that they themselves do not conduct the actual Risk Assessment. Business/ Functional Mangers perform the Risk and Impact Assessments for their lines of business. 50 to 100% of negative impacts such as poor press, fraud, trade conflicts, project recalls, being noncompetitive in international markets could have been mitigated with better Risk Management practices.

Less than 50% of the respondents agree or somewhat agree that that the Board in their organization is trained in Risk Management and understands its application to all business areas including marketing decisions, new products decisions, pandemic planning and international concerns. This same percentage also believe that Risk Managers make decisions based on experience, knowledge, written polices and regulations but less than 35% responded that data triangulation is used in their decision-making process.

Furthermore, less than 55% responded that Risk Management is part of their organizations culture, or that formal risk awareness training sessions are part of the onboarding process for new employees.

Relating to the Risk Managers reporting structure, the study finds out that less than 14% report to the Board, approximately 14% report to the CEO, less than 34% report to Senior Management, and in approximately 35% of the cases, the Risk

Manager is a position within other organization departments such as finance, marketing etc.

When asked about their organization's Pandemic preparedness plan, almost 55% responded that such scenarios were not considered as part of a risk assessment prior to Covid19. However, due to their policies and overall measures in place, almost 52% responded that their organization was prepared in advance for pandemic situations. 77% believe that going forward after Covid19, their Executive Management will require a fully documented pandemic plan to be maintained. Almost 60% responded that the Board should have ensured Pandemic Plans were in place prior to Covid19 and almost 40% responded that the Boards did not consider Pandemic Plans as part of their governance responsibility.

Summary of Research results

This subchapter summarizes what has been generally agreed upon by the Focus Group and Mass survey respondents – in conjunction with the implications of the literature review. If a Chief Risk Officer is identified, they are seen as business enablers, problem solvers and a resource to lean on. The role of the Risk Manager in the majority of organizations is providing oversight by reviewing the analysis done by project managers and business owners who are not trained in risk management processes. This oversight is mostly limited to areas such as Operations, while Business Continuity Managers and Information/Cyber Security Mangers work independently without oversight of the Risk Managers. Risk Managers are less often utilized in risk concerns in areas such as Marketing, Business Strategy, and International Business.

Of the Risk Managers who are identified by organizations to carry out the role, at least 30% are not formally trained and specialized. In addition, less than 50% of Boards are trained in Risk Management and understand its application to all business areas including marketing decisions new products decisions, pandemic planning and international concerns.

Over 45% organizations do not have a culture of risk awareness and do not have a formal risk awareness training session as part of their onboarding process. Even though the world has experienced pandemics in the past, over half of the organizations did not have pandemics as a consideration in their risk assessments. Prior to Covid19, over 40% of Boards did not consider it part of their responsibilities to ensure pandemics were part of their duties. Only slightly over half of the organizations were prepared to respond to a pandemic.

Conclusions and Recommendations

Research Question 1 What can Risk Managers do themselves to be better utilized?

In order to show the interrelation between the problem statement and the research results, this chapter is organized in such as way as to to congregate the answers based on the research questions; and consequently provide recommendations based on the results reached in this research.

Based on the published research regarding Risk Management in making major business decisions, I found that whereas there was a lot of debate regarding Risk Management in certain areas, the issue of making business decisions without utilizing Risk Management lacks proper attention. Corporations limit the use of Risk Management to common areas such as information technology, information security, production process, insurance and finance. The risk aspects of every area of the business including marketing, international business, human resources and others should be part of a formal risk process under the guise of a Risk Manager.

Risk Managers should conduct formal risk assessments and impact analysis of their corporations Risk Management structure and incorporate the entire operations of the business. Research showed that almost 70% believe that the majority of negative impacts such as poor press, fraud, trade conflicts, project recalls, and non-competitiveness in international markets could have been mitigated with better Risk Management practices.

The experience of the Risk Managers and how they trained for the position affects the utilization and their scope. The research showed that only just above 10% believe that their Risk Managers have formal training, approximately 70% believe that the Risk Managers have received their training from work or experience, while just below 20% responded they have no training at all.

When asked about the role and duties of the Risk Manager in their organization, in reference to the Risk Managers reporting structure, less than 14% report to the Board, less than 14% report to the CEO, less than 34% report to Senior Management, and approximately 35% is a position within other organization departments such as finance, marketing, etc.

Referencing the reporting structure, the Chief Risk Officer should be separate from the line areas and report to the Board or Senior Management as part of Corporate Governance, so they must have access to the Board as needed. The role of Risk Managers must be holistic, and trained Risk Managers who are placed under the Chief Risk Officer, should be more hands on with Enterprise Risk Management. Risk Management is such a field of specialization that there are Master's and PhD programs available in the field, because of the complexity and level of knowledge needed.

Research Question 2 Why are Risk Managers reviewing risk work done by others who are not trained instead of helping in the risk and impact analysis up front?

Early studies done after the 2007 financial crisis were recommending autonomy of Risk Managers from line management. Over time Risk Managers have become evaluators for proper analysis by operational areas. Their role should include advising Executives and the Board regarding evolving areas of risk that need attention. Since operational mangers certainly deal on a day to day basis with operational risks, they should still be included in the process - but also trained appropriately. Having (junior) Risk Managers work with the operational areas and giving guidance as to risk areas not being considered and conducting full Risk Management processes that they are trained in, would be a great asset to the line manager. These Risk Managers should report to the Chief Risk Office and not to the lines, though.

The research results showed that almost 40% believe that the Risk Officer provides oversight to drive risk capabilities in constantly changing environments. They also felt that since there are so many compliance requirements the risk manager is ensuring consistency of practice of the enterprise areas that are conducting the risk assessments. Another 40% believe that if their industry does not have compliance requirements, the result is that no is placed in charge of Risk Management for the entire organization.

While all managers are expected to consider risk, and in many companies the Project Mangers conduct a risk assessment, they are not necessarily trained in Risk Management. Formal project management risk training pertains most often to the success of the project being completed and implemented. the Project Manager training does not expand to considering risk after it is in production and out in the world.

Many organizations, where enterprise Risk Assessments and Risk Analysis are not conducted by trained Risk Managers, are often more concerned with meeting compliance than identifying the actual risks that could impact the organization both quantitatively and qualitatively. Qualitatively, it could include loss of customers, loss of reputation, loss of image, customer dissatisfaction, employee morale, and many more. Quantitively, it can include costs related to decrease in stock, regulatory fines, legal fees, and more.

Mangers who are not trained in risk management and are affiliated to specific functional area of the organization, who are conducting the risk assessments and impact analysis, are so closely related to the operations of the area, that they often can't look at the risks objectively.

A Risk Management area that includes risk outside of just the financial risk and insurance risk should be part of every organization. It should be run by a Chief Risk Officer and be made up of trained Risk Managers.

Research Question 3 Instead of management simply telling business units to consider risks, why don't they have a requirement to have a Risk Manager conduct risk assessment for all new projects that can have negative impacts to the business?

Major new project risks which are determined by the operational areas are reviewed by the Chief information Officer. The problem is that risks affect all areas of the Corporation, not just new projects. This thesis shows that Enterprise Risk Management should span throughout the enterprise, yet the studies on which the organizations have based their risk structure model on, were focusing on only one area of the risk discipline, to determine how Risk Management is being handled. The general Risk Mangers themselves were not included. Risk areas such as finance, information security, business continuity and other specialized risk areas were each separate studies and the results were being applied across the entire corporation, even though the entire organization was not considered in the analysis.

In response to questions 3 reference Risk Managers conducting the risk assessments, the research showed that less than 40% of risk and impact assessments are conducted by a Risk Manager. Approximately 50% responded that Risk Managers make decisions on such areas as experience, knowledge, written polices and regulations. Less than 35% responded that data triangulation is used.

Instead of management simply telling business units to consider risks, why don't they have a requirement to have a Risk Manager conduct risk assessment for all new projects that can have negative impacts to the business?

In response to questions 3 reference Risk Managers reviewing risk assessments instead of doing them, almost 40% review the assessments for new projects but not necessarily operational risks as well. In other organizations, project managers, functional and business area managers tend to conduct their own assessments, often so without possessing formal training. Less than 20% of Business Managers were formally trained in performing a risk and impact assessment. In addition, only just over 40% of Boards review the operational risks of the organization.

The focus group results showed that almost 90% of mangers in operations and enterprise risk areas believe that having the Risk Manager on projects is an asset. Yet the research shows that 40% of risk and impact assessments are done without Risk Managers whose help would have benefited the organizations. This shows that the scope of Risk Managers even in new projects should be expanded further.

On another note, governance should include Enterprise Risk Management regardless whether an organization has compliance responsibilities or not. The image of the company, loss of clients, loss of faith in the company, and more are at risk.

The respondents reported that less than 50% of the organizations were prepared for a pandemic such as the

Covid19 Pandemic. The scope of Risk Managers should change to one of being more actively involved and as an advisor than of one of checking to make sure that something looks good on paper.

Covid19, proved that not considering pandemics in Risk Assessments and Risk Analyses caused negative impacts for many organizations. Organizations in which Risk Managers were considering risks from an enterprise level and have taken into account past risks such as SARS and other pandemics, were better prepared. Nevertheless, there is no doubt that the Covid19 pandemic will shape organizational decisions regarding Risk Management in the coming years.

Bibliography

1. Aebi, V., Sabato, G. and Schmid, M., 2012. Risk management, corporate governance, and bank performance in the financial crisis. *Journal of Banking & Finance*, [online] 36(12), pp.3213-3226. Available at: <https://www.sciencedirect.com/science/article/abs/pii/S0378426611003104> [Accessed 19 August 2020].

2. Alam, A. and Ali Shah, S., 2013. Corporate Governance and Its Impact on Firm Risk. *SSRN Electronic Journal*,

3. Al-Thani, F. and Merna, T., 2008. *Corporate Risk Management*. 2nd ed. Hoboken, N.J.: Wiley, p.3.

4. Andrews, P. and Manes, S., 1992. *I Blew It, Perot Says -- He Didn't Buy Up Microsoft When He Had A Chance In '79 | The Seattle Times*. [online] Archive.seattletimes.com. Available at: <https://archive.seattletimes.com/archive/?date=19920614&slug=1497096> [Accessed 2 February 2020].

5. Appolonia, A., 2019. *How Blackberry Went From Controlling The Smartphone Market To A Phone Of The Past*. [online] Business Insider. Available at: <https://www.businessinsider.com/blackberry-smartphone-rise-fall-mobile-failure-innovate-2019-11> [Accessed 22 December 2019].

6. Ariz, N., Manab, N. and Othman, S., 2015. Exploring the perspectives of corporate governance and theories on sustainability risk management (SRM). *Asian Economic and Financial Review*, [online] (5(10), pp.1148-1158. Available at: <Retrieved from https://search.proquest.com/docview/1739300987?accountid=191083> [Accessed 22 December 2019].

7. Becker, S., 2019. *Https://Www.Usatoday.Com/Story/Money/Business/2014/12/20/Cheat-Sheet-Business-Blunders/20627213/*. [online] Usatoday.com. Available at: <https://www.usatoday.com/story/money/business/2014/12/20/cheat-sheet-business-blunders/20627213/> [Accessed 17 November 2019].

8. Berman, M., 2019. *3 Reasons Chief Risk Officers Fail | Ncontracts*. [online] Ncontracts. Available at: <https://ncontracts.com/articles/3-reasons-chief-risk-officers-fail/> [Accessed 15 December 2019].

9. Boyd, W., Beck, U. and Shrader-Frechette, K., 1993. Risk Society: Towards a New Modernity. *Economic Geography*, 69(4), p.432.

10. Carrel, P., 2012. *The Handbook of Risk Management [Electronic Resource]: Implementing A Post-Crisis Corporate Culture*. John Wiley & Sons, pp.2, 67.

11. Chief-risk-officer.com. 2019. *International Association of Risk and Compliance Professionals (IARCP)*. [online] Available at: <https://www.chief-risk-officer.com/> [Accessed 26 December 2019].

12. Chief-risk-officer.com. n.d. *International Association of Risk and Compliance Professionals (IARCP)*. [online] Available at: <https://www.chief-risk-officer.com/> [Accessed 15 December 2019].

13. Crouhy, M., Galai, D. and Mark, R., 2014. *The Essentials of Risk Management, Second Edition, 2Nd Edition*. 2nd ed. New York: McGraw Hill Education, pp.609-618.

14. Danisman, G. and Demirel, P., 2019. Corporate risk management practices and firm value in an emerging market: a mixed methods approach. *Risk Management*, 21(1), pp.19-47.

15. Do, H., Railwaywalla, M. and Thayer, J., 2016. [online] Erm.ncsu.edu. Available at: <https://erm.ncsu.edu/az/erm/i/chan/library/Integration_of_ERM_and_Strategy_Case_Study.pdf> [Accessed 25 January 2020].

16. Ellyatt, H., 2020. *Climate Change Leads The Davos Agenda, But It's Not Even A Top 10 Risk For Ceos*. [online] CNBC. Available at: <https://www.cnbc.com/2020/01/21/davos-climate-change-and-ceos.html> [Accessed 1 February 2020].

17. Erm.ncsu.edu. 2019. *Strengthening the Role of The Chief Risk Officer in An Organization - ERM - Enterprise Risk Management Initiative | North Carolina State Poole College of Management.* [online] Available at: <https://erm.ncsu.edu/library/article/strengthening-the-role-of-the-chief-risk-officer-in-an-organization/> [Accessed 21 December 2019].

18. Erm.ncsu.edu. 2019. *Top Risks Report 2020: Executive Perspectives on Top Risks For 2020 - ERM - Enterprise Risk Management Initiative | North Carolina State Poole College of Management.* [online] Available at: <https://erm.ncsu.edu/library/article/top-risks-report-2020-executive-perspectives> [Accessed 21 December 2019].

19. Gates, S., Nicolas, J. and Walker, P., 2012. The Effect of Psychological Safety and Leadership Style on Risk Performance with Enterprise Risk Management as Intervening Variables. *European Journal of Business and Management*, VOL. 13(NO. 3).

20. Gatzert, N. and Schmit, J., 2016. Supporting strategic success through enterprise-wide reputation risk management. *The Journal of Risk Finance*, 17(1), pp.26-45.

21. Gennari, F., Gandini, G. and Cassano, R., 2014. Global Responsibility and Strategic Risk Management. *Journal of Business Management and*

Applied Economics, [online] III. Available at:
<https://d1wqtxts1xzle7.cloudfront.net/42827465/Glob
al_Responsibility_and_Strategic_Risk20160219-8463-
1qbrw0n.pdf?1455869509=&response-content-
disposition=inline%3B+filename%3DGlobal_Respons
ibility_and_Strategic_Risk.pdf&Expires=1598825186
&Signature=gTTTcry6tyTMpHFUeXtyWsB4IWf0Nn
2taRDERO84IKF9olt-
ivsrpOBPt14HPu5gGXCfMBBc8qfqA2rxO-
n1b5GaKSIYPkqWkxlaOXpA8HgxpkYRAowb2Fraj
G9-ahqphGz8IwT-Xl-
JepS8q9gkxA~5~i6EsE1yLIrufuQQPWiJhVHnPeU0u
ZXXX0s~N1DawZeWwJkLcb6ou3HXDjAW1rQ8jT8
Y-
eYtrjE0ofVFyMRIGLZWeHbHBOTngS3IrFtOxz84W
yGiAa1rVzbEV7T682buSHyzvcIcPowqqkBsbKuXK
YVGjd-
YYJRGP7qAmYDkQ~aUEGpV1kiM4M5jDfOflw__
&Key-Pair-Id=APKAJLOHF5GGSLRBV4ZA>
[Accessed 15 December 2019].

22. Goncalves, M. and Xia, H., 2015. *Comparing Emerging and Advanced Markets*. 1st ed. New York: Business Expert Press, pp.81-110.

23. Gontarek, W. and Belghitar, Y., 2018. Risk governance: Examining its impact upon bank performance and risk-taking. *Financial Markets, Institutions & Instruments*, 27(5), pp.187-224.

24. Green, P., 2015. *Risk Management: A Common Framework for The Entire Organization*. Oxford: Elsevier Science & Technology, p.vii-xii.

25. Groysberg, B. and Slind, M., 2012. *The Silent Killer of Big Companies*. [online] Harvard Business Review. Available at: <https://hbr.org/2012/10/the-silent-killer-of-big-companies> [Accessed 23 January 2020].

26. Haasch, P., 2019. *New Coke Is The Weirdest Pop Culture Throwback In Stranger Things 3*. [online] Polygon. Available at: <https://www.polygon.com/2019/7/6/20683542/stranger-things-3-new-coke-1985-coca-cola-where-to-buy> [Accessed 18 August 2020].

27. Hassan, A. and Yawer, T., 2013. Analysis of Risk Management Practices in Business Enterprises of Pakistan. *Global Management Journal for Academic & Corporate Studies*, 3(1), pp.45-61.

28. Hillson, D., 2019. *Risk Management: Best Practice and Future Developments*. [online] Journal.iaccm.com. Available at: <https://journal.iaccm.com/contracting-excellence-journal/risk-management-best-practice-and-future-developments> [Accessed 15 December 2019].

29. History.state.gov. 2020. *Milestones: 1801–1829 - Office of The Historian*. [online] Available at: <https://history.state.gov/milestones/1801-1829/napoleonic-wars> [Accessed 17 August 2020].

30. Ho, V., 2012. Corporate Governance as Risk Regulation in China: A Comparative View of Risk Oversight, Risk Management, and Accountability. *European Journal of Risk Regulation*, 3(4), pp.463-475.

31. Hodge, N., 2019. *Learning From Corporate Collapse – Risk Management*. [online] Rmmagazine.com. Available at: <http://www.rmmagazine.com/2019/02/01/learning-from-corporate-collapse/> [Accessed 2 February 2020].

32. Hofstede, G., 1984. *Culture's Consequences, International Differences in Work-Related Values*. 1st ed. Beverly Hills: Sage.

33. Hofstede, G., 2005. *Cultures Consequences*. 2nd ed. Thousand Oaks, Calif.: Sage Publications.

34. Hopkin, P., 2018. *Fundamentals of Risk Management*. 5th ed. New York: Kerogen page Limited, pp.43-51.

35. International Finance Corporation, 2012. *Standards on Risk Governance in Financial Institutions*. International Finance Corporation.

36. Isaca.org. n.d. *About ISACA*. [online] Available at: <https://www.isaca.org/about-isaca/Pages/default.aspx> [Accessed 22 December 2019].

37. ISO. 2019. *ISO 31000 Risk Management*. [online] Available at: <https://www.iso.org/iso-31000-risk-management.html> [Accessed 17 November 2019].

38. Kaplan, R. and Mikes, A., 2012. *Managing Risks: A New Framework*. [online] Harvard Business Review. Available at: <https://hbr.org/2012/06/managing-risks-a-new-framework> [Accessed 18 November 2019].

39. Keaton (Reviewer), W., 2019. *How Enterprise Risk Management (ERM) Works*. [online] Investopedia. Available at: <https://www.investopedia.com/terms/e/enterprise-risk-management.asp> [Accessed 15 December 2019].

40. Levin, A., 1999. Risk managers urged to broaden outlook. *National Underwriter*, (vol. 103, no. 45), p.9.

41. Louisot, J., 2015. RISK AND/OR RESILIENCE MANAGEMENT. *Risk Governance and Control: Financial Markets & Institutions*, 5(2).

42. Lubber, M., 2019. *At Exxon, A Failure Of Governance On Climate Risk*. [online] Forbes.com. Available at: <https://www.forbes.com/sites/mindylubber/2019/05/23/at-exxon-a-failure-of-governance-on-climate-risk/#2f7014ec3cc9> [Accessed 24 January 2020].

43. Majdalawieh, M. and Gammack, J., 2015. RISK MANAGEMENT PRACTICES IN A RAPIDLY

DEVELOPING ECONOMY: THE CASE OF THE UAE. *Internal Auditing*, vol. 30(2), pp.pp. 24-35.

44. McCafferty, J., 2016. *How Silos Can Cause Risk-Management Headaches*. [online] Misti.com. Available at: <https://misti.com/internal-audit-insights/how-silos-can-cause-risk-management-headaches> [Accessed 24 January 2020].

45. McCullough, B., 2014. *The Real Reason Excite Turned Down Buying Google For $750,000 In 1999*. [online] Internet History Podcast. Available at: <http://www.internethistorypodcast.com/2014/11/the-real-reason-excite-turned-down-buying-google-for-750000-in-1999/> [Accessed 2 February 2020].

46. McShane, M., 2018. Enterprise risk management: history and a design science proposal. *The Journal of Risk Finance*, 19(2), pp.137-153.

47. McShane, M., 2018. Enterprise risk management: history and a design science proposal. *The Journal of Risk Finance*, 19(2), pp.137-153.

48. Meidell, A. and Kaarbøe, K., 2017. How the enterprise risk management function influences decision-making in the organization – A field study of a large, global oil and gas company. *The British Accounting Review*, 49(1), pp.39-55.

49. Meulbroek, L., 2002. A SENIOR MANAGER'S GUIDE TO INTEGRATED RISK MANAGEMENT. *Journal of Applied Corporate Finance*, 14(4), pp.56-70.

50. Meyer, H. and Ujah, N., 2017. Managed earnings: The negative impact of marketer's discretionary advertising expenditures on firm performance. *Marketing Intelligence & Planning*, 35(2), pp.192-204.

51. Na.theiia.org. 2013. *IIA POSITION PAPER: THE THREE LINES OF DEFENSE IN EFFECTIVE RISK MANAGEMENT AND CONTROL.* [online] Available at: <http://na.theiia.org/standards-guidance/Public%20Documents/PP%20The%20Three%20Lines%20of%20Defense%20in%20Effective%20Risk%20Management%20and%20Control.pdf> [Accessed 14 December 2019].

52. Pelzer, P., 2009. The displaced world of risk: risk management as alienated risk (perception?). *Society and Business Review*, 4(1), pp.26-36.

53. Pernell, K., Jung, J. and Dobbin, F., 2017. The Hazards of Expert Control: Chief Risk Officers and Risky Derivatives. *American Sociological Review*, 82(3), pp.511-541.

54. Pernell, K., Jung, J. and Dobbin, F., 2019. *Research: Hiring Chief Risk Officers Led Banks To Take On Even More Risk.* [online] Harvard Business Review.

Available at: <https://hbr.org/2017/07/research-hiring-chief-risk-officers-led-banks-to-take-on-even-more-risk> [Accessed 14 December 2019].

55. Phillips, S., 2011. *Executive - Executive Insight.* [online] Executive. Available at: <https://web.archive.org/web/20111114213418/http://www.executive-magazine.com/getarticle.php?article=14802> [Accessed 15 February 2020].

56. Phillips, S., 2019. *Executive Perspective On Top Risks In 2020 - Key Issues Being Discussed In The Boardroom And C -Suite.* [online] Erm.ncsu.edu. Available at: <https://erm.ncsu.edu/az/erm/i/chan/library/2020-erm-execs-top-risks-report.pdf> [Accessed 15 December 2019].

57. Poole College North Carolina State of Management, 2019. *Executive Perspectives on Top Risks 2020 - Key Issues Being Discussed.* [online] ERM. Available at: <https://erm.ncsu.edu/az/erm/i/chan/library/2020-erm-execs-top-risks-report.pdf> [Accessed 1 September 2020].

58. Pouzar, E., 1993. Benchmarking fad lures risk managers' bosses. *National Underwriter*, (vol. 97, no. 7), p.7.

59. Power, M., 2009. The risk management of nothing. *Accounting, Organizations and Society*, [online] 34(6-7), pp.849-855. Available at: <https://doi.org/10.1016/j.aos.2009.06.001> [Accessed 7 December 2019].

60. Power, M., Ashby, S. and Palermo, T., 2012. *Risk Culture in Financial Organizations A Research Report*. [online] Lse.ac.uk. Available at: <http://www.lse.ac.uk/accounting/assets/CARR/docum ents/Risk-Culture-in-Financial-Organisations/Final-Risk-Culture-Report.pdf> [Accessed 26 January 2020].

61. Press, A., 2019. *Coca-Cola Is Bringing Back The Failed New Coke Recipe In Honor Of 'Stranger Things'*. [online] MarketWatch. Available at: <https://www.marketwatch.com/story/coca-cola-is-bringing-back-the-failed-new-coke-recipe-in-honor-of-stranger-things-2019-05-21> [Accessed 2 February 2020].

62. PWC, 2016. [online] Coso.org. Available at: <https://www.coso.org/Documents/COSO-ERM-draft-Post-Exposure-Version.pdf> [Accessed 21 January 2020].

63. PWC, 2019. [online] Pwc.com. Available at: <https://www.pwc.com/gx/en/ceo-survey/2019/report/pwc-22nd-annual-global-ceo-survey.pdf> [Accessed 2 February 2020].

64. Qed.qld.gov.au. 2019. *Enterprise Risk Management Framework.* [online] Available at: <https://qed.qld.gov.au/publications/management-and-frameworks/enterprise-risk-management-framework> [Accessed 7 November 2019].

65. Roberthalf.com.au. 2019. *Risk Management Job Description and Duties | Robert Half.* [online] Available at: <https://www.roberthalf.com.au/our-services/financial-services/risk-management-jobs> [Accessed 17 November 2019].

66. Sammer, J., Witt, K. and Bacon, P., 2015. *8 Best Practices for Aligning Strategy, Planning, And Risk.* [online] FM Magazine. Available at: <https://www.fm-magazine.com/issues/2015/may/strategy-planning-risk-best-practices.html> [Accessed 25 May 2015].

67. Sax, J. and Andersen, T., 2018. Making Risk Management Strategic: Integrating Enterprise Risk Management with Strategic Planning. *European Management Review*, 16(3), pp.719-740.

68. Sax, J. and Andersen, T., 2018. Making Risk Management Strategic: Integrating Enterprise Risk Management with Strategic Planning. *European Management Review*, 16(3), pp.719-740.

69. Servaes, H., Tamayo, A. and Tufano, P., 2009. The Theory and Practice of Corporate Risk

Management*. *Journal of Applied Corporate Finance*, 21(4), pp.60-78.

70. Servaes, H., Tamayo, A. and Tufano, P., 2009. The Theory and Practice of Corporate Risk Management*. *Journal of Applied Corporate Finance*, 21(4), pp.60-78.

71. Shimizu, T., Park, Y. and Choi, S., 2014. Project managers and risk management: A comparative study between Japanese and Korean firms. *International Journal of Production Economics*, 147, pp.437-447.

72. Snyder, C., 2019. *Do Risk Committees Improve Strategic Risk Management?* [online] The National Law Review. Available at: <https://www.natlawreview.com/article/do-risk-committees-improve-strategic-risk-management> [Accessed 14 December 2019].

73. Stein, M., 2016. *Chief Risk Officers Are Taking On A Broader Role*. [online] WSJ. Available at: <https://blogs.wsj.com/riskandcompliance/2016/04/01/chief-risk-officers-are-taking-on-a-broader-role/> [Accessed 15 December 2019].

74. Stulz, R., 2019. Six Ways Companies Mismanage Risk. *Harvard Business Review*, [online] Available at: <https://hbr.org/2009/03/six-ways-companies-mismanage-risk> [Accessed 7 December 2019].

75. Tayon, B., 2019. *The Wells Fargo Cross-Selling Scandal*. [online] Corpgov.law.harvard.edu. Available at: <https://corpgov.law.harvard.edu/2019/02/06/the-wells-fargo-cross-selling-scandal-2/> [Accessed 26 January 2020].

76. The National Law Review. 2019. *How A Strong(Er) SRM Program Could Have Helped Boeing*. [online] Available at: <https://www.natlawreview.com/article/how-stronger-srm-program-could-have-helped-boeing> [Accessed 14 December 2019].

77. Twin, A., 2020. *How The Delphi Method Works*. [online] Investopedia. Available at: <https://www.investopedia.com/terms/d/delphi-method.asp> [Accessed 24 September 2020].

78. Wall Street Journal, 2019. Looking for Business Growth? Appoint a CRO. [online] Available at: <https://deloitte.wsj.com/riskandcompliance/2019/09/02/looking-for-business-growth-appoint-a-cro/> [Accessed 15 September 2019].

79. Webb, R., 2019. The Top 8 Risks to Manage in 2019. [Blog] *RISK MANAGEMENT BLOG - CLEARRISK*, Available at: <https://www.clearrisk.com/risk-management-blog/top-risks-2019> [Accessed 30 October 2019].

80. Wolke, T., 2017. *Risk Management*. Walter de Gruyter GmbH, p.v.

81. Woods, M., 2011. *Risk Management in Organizations: An Integrated Case Study Approach*. London and New York: Routledge Taylor & Francis Group, p.155.

Annexes

Annex 1 – Targeted Survey

Delphi Survey - findings

75% responded a Risk Manager was fully utilized in Operations.

62% responded a Risk Manager was fully utilized in Information/Cyber Security

50% responded a Risk Manager was fully utilized in Marketing

50% responded a Risk Manager was fully utilized in Business Continuity

Less than 50% responded a Risk Manager was fully utilized in Business Strategy, International Business and Disaster Recovery.

While almost 40% responded that:

> *When an individual is named for a Risk Manger position, the reach of the authority tends to be very large as most organizations are falling behind their compliance obligations due to the ever-increasing number of laws that must be followed and considered, from registering to lobbyist registry to managing information security. The Risk Officer is an*

interdepartmental business enabler, problem solver and resource in times of uncertainty. Work with process owners and managers to mitigate risk. (find solutions and implement) Process owners are responsible for implementation. The Risk Officer establishes the oversight, control and discipline to drive continuous improvement of an entity's Risk Management capabilities in a constantly changing operating environment. Responsible for knowing the system and the processes and understanding the risks associated Evaluating Risk Management planning to ensure consistency and accuracy of practice; Facilitating and driving risk management capability

Almost 40% responded that:

There is no one in charge of Risk Management specifically. There are no legislative requirements in our industry to manage risks and conduct audits. Focused on financial risk, and compliance risks. This is how they interpreted the legislation that requires Risk Management committees, even though there is no exclusion for information security and data protection. There is no definition or job description for Risk Manager at our company. There is no official job description for risk management. All managers and all staff are expected to actively participate in the management of risk. They actively identify, communicate and respond to expected, emerging or changing risks; Contribute to the process of developing

*Risk Management plans for their state or branch';
Implement and monitor risk plans within their area of
responsibility*

Details of Focus Group Questionnaire Survey 1

The synopsis of replies to the questions asked were:

1. **What is a common definition or job description of a Risk Manager in your organization?**
   a. Identify and assess risks to policy/program delivery and/or compliance with legislation/regulation/government policy, provide advice to decision makers on required management/mitigation strategies, and monitor implementation.
   b. Establishes the oversight, control and discipline to drive continuous improvement of an entity's Risk Management capabilities in a constantly changing operating environment.
   c. Responsible for knowing the system and the processes and understanding the risks associated.
   d. The Risk Manager is an interdepartmental business enabler, problem solver and resource in times of uncertainty.
   e. Work with process owners and managers to mitigate risk. (find solutions and implement) Process owner responsible for implementation
   f. There is no definition or job description for Risk Manager at our company. In fact, risks are managed through the CISO. We do a Chief Privacy Officer, but he is a lawyer largely involved in working with client and does not effectively oversees any Risk Management activities. The work performed by our

CISO and her technical team is overseen by the Information Security Governance Committee. I represent the Montreal HQ in this committee and provide several suggestions to improve Risk Management activities within the firm. However, there is no official job description for risk management.

g. There is no one in charge of Risk Management specifically. There are no legislative requirements in our industry to manage risks and conduct audits. Focused on financial risk, and compliance risks. This is how they interpreted the legislation that requires Risk Management committees, even though there is no exclusion for information security and data protection.

h. Chief Risk and Compliance officers are in charge of overseeing compliance with applicable law, and the legal as well as HR department reports to this individual. They are responsible for identifying and analyzing risks the organization faces across all our businesses and operations. In my experience, and based on my involvement with our Risk Management teams, the role has traditionally focused on raising awareness and visibility of individual risks, particularly at the board level.

i. This is not a strict title we use – closest relevant description is: All staff: All staff are expected to actively participate in the management of risk.

In addition to specific responsibilities assigned to them, staff should: Actively identify, communicate and respond to expected, emerging or changing risks; Contribute to the process of developing Risk Management plans for their state or branch'; Implement and monitor risk plans within their area of responsibility. □ Director Risk Section: Responsibilities include: Facilitate, challenge and drive the development of the AEC's Risk Management framework; Coordinating the implementation of the AEC Risk Management framework; Evaluating Risk Management planning to ensure consistency and accuracy of practice; Facilitating and driving risk management capability within the agency; Reporting to senior managers at regular intervals; Coordinating Risk Management capability training for all staff;

j. Ensuring employees receive support in fulfilling their Risk Management responsibilities.

k. Risk Manager works under Work Health and Safety. Business Continuity Manager works under Security

Respondent Observations

Overtime, the reach of its functions included most departments, as they all had issues managing risks, and the deployment of the ISMS and related policies also involved this person. Project managers were eventually assigned to this person as well. Therefore, I noticed that when an individual is named for this position, the reach of the authority tend to be very large as most organizations are falling behind their compliance obligations due to the ever increasing number of laws that must be followed and considered, from registering to lobbyist registry to managing information security.

2. Is a Risk Manager utilized to assist with strategies and decisions in the following areas?

	Yes	**No**	**Limited**	**N/A**
Operations	6	2		
International Business	3	3	1	1
Marketing	4	4		
Business Strategy	3	1	4	
Information/Cyber Security	5	2	1	
Business Continuity	4	2	2	
Disaster Recovery	3	3	2	

3. Is the perception of Managers in the areas listed in question 3 that having the Risk Manager on projects a hindrance or a help?

    a. The interface does not occur at the "Manager" level rather the interface occurs with the VP, SVP, and EVP levels. These VPs, SVPs, and EVPs definitely see the Risk Manager as a help not a hindrance.

    b. Variable – most managers accept there is a role for Risk Management as part of their work. They may handle their risk assessments without inputs form the Risk Manager.

c. In some cases, it is viewed as a help as escalated awareness may be leveraged to obtain more resources or establish compliance requirements

d. Depends – normally the Project Manager for the project handles the risk assessment. In rare cases the project will ask my role to assist with an initial risk assessment workshop, in which case it is desired for, and therefore considered helpful.

e. Predominately a help. There is an expectation from our organization's executive leadership that risks are identified and managed in the course of business. Areas will often seek specialized assistance to meet this expectation.

4. What prevents managers in the areas listed in question 3 from requesting the Risk manager to help/advise on projects?

a. In our organization, ERM (and the Risk Manager) is taken very seriously and seen as a way to both achieve and maintain competitive advantage

b. Nothing. All they need to do is ask. That responded, they all have "day jobs" and focusing on Risk Management may not be at the forefront of their minds until ERM comes knocking on their door.

c. Too busy or they may not know the Risk Manager. Risk culture is a part of our businesses and has been for many years

d. Nothing; just haven't done it
e. A lack of awareness or understanding about the Risk Management role.
f. No actual hindrance —mostly a lack of desire to do so – either because they consider they already have the skills in the project team to identify and manage risks, or due to a lack of engagement with the Risk Management discipline.
g. A perception that time constraints limit/prevent the ability to seek assistance to assess risks.

Details of the Focus Group Questionnaire Survey 2

The following questions were based on the synopsis of the first survey. The participants of the first two surveys where the same 8 individuals in the Focus Group since this was based on the Delphi Methodology.

I provided a questionnaire survey to a focus group made up of 8 Risk Mangers compromising both Chief Risk Officers and Enterprise Risk Managers.

Instructions to participants:

Please circle the letter for each question that you most closely agree with.

1. **What is a common definition or job description of a Risk Manager in your organization?**
   a. Chief Risk and Compliance officers oversee compliance with applicable law, and the legal as well as HR department reports to this individual. They are responsible for identifying and analyzing risks the organization faces across all our businesses and operations. The role has traditionally focused on raising awareness and visibility of individual risks, particularly at the board level. They identify and assess risks to policy/program delivery and/or compliance with legislation/regulation/government policy, provide advice to decision makers on required management/mitigation strategies, and monitor implementation. The Risk Manager

responsibilities include: Facilitate, challenge and drive the development of the Risk Management framework; Coordinating the implementation of the Risk Management framework

Selected by 2 of the 8

b. When an individual is named for this position, the reach of the authority tends to be very large as most organizations are falling behind their compliance obligations due to the ever-increasing number of laws that must be followed and considered, from registering to lobbyist registry to managing information security. The Risk Officer is an interdepartmental business enabler, problem solver and resource in times of uncertainty. Work with process owners and managers to mitigate risk. (find solutions and implement) Process owners are responsible for implementation. The Risk Officer establishes the oversight, control and discipline to drive continuous improvement of an entity's Risk Management capabilities in a constantly changing operating environment. Responsible for knowing the system and the processes and understanding the risks associated Evaluating Risk Management planning to ensure consistency and accuracy of practice; Facilitating and driving risk management capability

Selected by 3 of the 8

c. There is no one in charge of Risk Management specifically. There are no legislative requirements in

our industry to manage risks and conduct audits. Focused on financial risk, and compliance risks. This is how they interpreted the legislation that requires Risk Management committees, even though there is no exclusion for information security and data protection. There is no definition or job description for Risk Manager at our company. There is no official job description for risk management. All managers and all staff are expected to actively participate in the management of risk. They actively identify, communicate and respond to expected, emerging or changing risks; Contribute to the process of developing Risk Management plans for their state or branch'; Implement and monitor risk plans within their area of responsibility
Selected by 3 of the 8

2. **Is the perception of Mangers in operations and ERM risk areas that having the Risk Manager on projects a hindrance or a help?**
   a. Hindrance
   Selected by 1 of the 8
   b. Help
   Selected by 7 of the 8

3. **What prevents managers from requesting the Risk manager to help/advise on projects?**
   a. They do risk managers are taken very seriously and seen to both achieve and maintain competitive advantage

Selected by 1 of the 8

b. A lack of awareness or understanding about the Risk Management role.

Selected by 4 of the 8

c. A perception that time constraints limit/prevent the ability to seek assistance to assess risks.

Selected by 3 of the 8

Annex 2 – Mass Survey

An overview of the Mass Survey

Survey 3 was answered by 68 top tier managers and auditors.

- Approximately 70% at least somewhat believe Risk Managers utilized throughout their organization are formally trained and specialized.
- Almost 62% believe the Risk Mangers only review the Risk Assessments done by Project Managers, Functional and Business area and that they themselves do not conduct the actual Risk Assessment. Business/ Functional Mangers perform the Risk and Impact Assessments for their lines of business.
- Only just above 10% believe that their Risk Managers have formal training, approximately 70% believe that the Risk Managers have received their training from work or experience, while just below 20% responded they have no training at all.
- Less than 50% responded they agree or somewhat agree that that their Board is trained in Risk Management and understands its application to all business areas including marketing decisions new products decisions, pandemic planning and international concerns.
- Almost 70% responded that at least 50 to 100% of negative impacts such as poor press, fraud, trade conflicts, project recalls, being noncompetitive in international markets could have been mitigated with better Risk Management practices,.

- Approximately 50% responded that Risk Managers make decisions on such areas as experience, knowledge, written polices and regulations. Less than 35% responded that data triangulation is used.
- Less than 55% responded that Risk Management is part of their organizations culture and less than 45% responded that formal risk awareness training sessions are part of the onboarding process for new employees.
- As far as the Risk Managers reporting structure, less than 14% report to the Board, less than 14% report to the CEO, less than 34% report to Senior Management, and approximately 35% is a position within other organization departments such as finance, marketing, etc.
- Refence Pandemic preparation, almost 55% responded that it was not considered as part of a risk assessment prior to COVID 19. However, almost 52% responded their organization was prepared in advance for pandemics.
- Most believe going forward, their Executive Management will require a fully documented pandemic plan to be maintained. Almost 60% responded that the Board should have ensured Pandemic Plans were in place prior to Coronavirus and almost 40% responded that the Boards did not consider Pandemic Plans as part of their governance responsibility.

Detailed results from the Mass Survey (part 1)

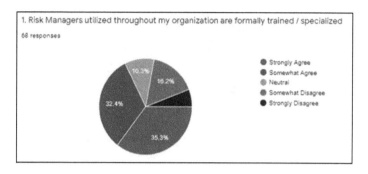

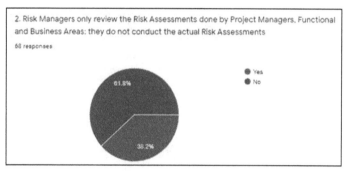

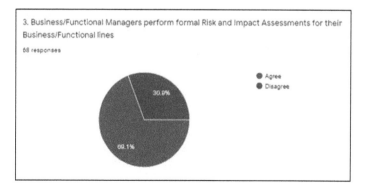

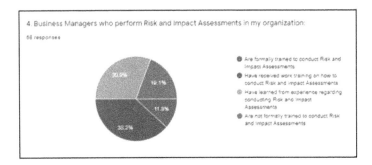

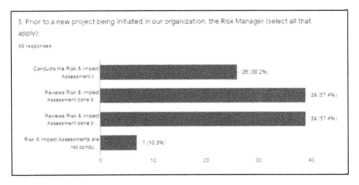

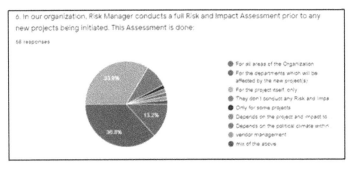

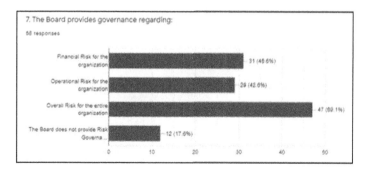

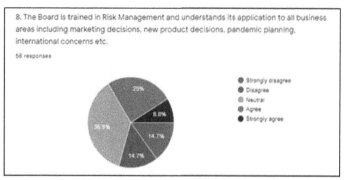

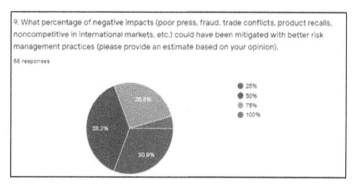

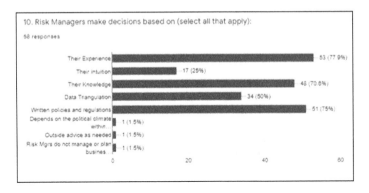

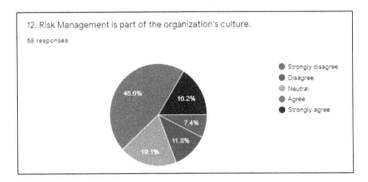

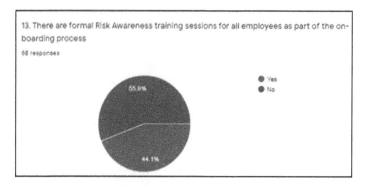

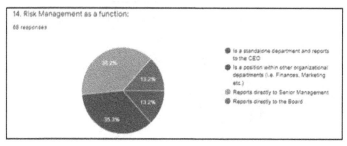

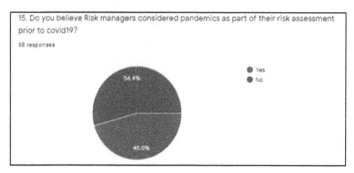

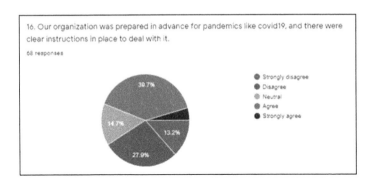

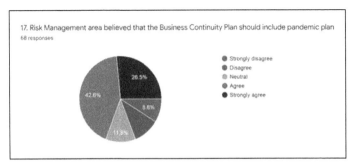

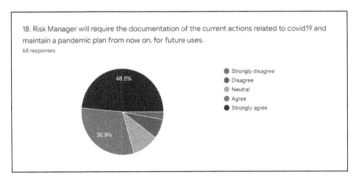

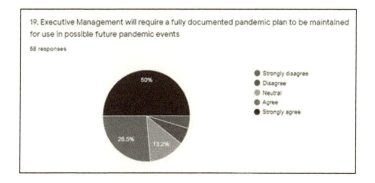

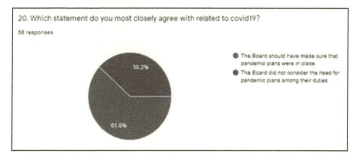

Dear Reader,

Thank you so much for going on the journey of Navigating the Shifting Landscape and the Evolving Roles of Chief Information Security Officers (CISO's) and Chief Risk Officers (CRO's) with me. I wish you continued success in the field.

Michael

Contact the Author

Dr. Michael C. Redmond, PhD

Connect with me on LinkedIn
LinkedIn Profile
https://www.linkedin.com/in/michaelredmondphd

Continued Learning with
Dr. Michael C. Redmond, PhD

Disaster Recovery Institute allows 20 Continuing Education Units for completion of this Audio training Course.

Online: https://www.redmondworldwide.org/

~~$395.00~~

Order under tab "Educational Audio Training"

For you, as a gift for reading this book, it is only $300.00 plus shipping.

Use code: CISO/CRO Book

Or simply call Fred at +1 (213) 718-7303 and tell him that you read **CSIO/CRO Thesis Book** and would like the discount applied. He will be happy to take your order over the phone. (Ask about additional discounts for orders of 10 or more).

Special Offer Audio Training Program

Use code: *CSIO/CRO Book*

Online price: ~~$395.00~~

Discounted price only: *$300.00* plus Shipping

(Call for additional discounts for 10 or more)

Call: +1 (213) 718-7303,   What App: +1 (213) 718-7303

https//:www.rwknowledge.com

- **20 CEU from DRII for Business Continuity Management**

- **Audio Training with Workbook**

Michael's Published Books

Mastering Business Continuity Management

Disasters, including technological, natural, and manmade, have increased exponentially, making this book essential for organizations and students in areas such as Business Management, Business Continuity, Disaster Recovery, Information Security, Risk Management, Project Management, Audit, Compliance, and IT.

This book takes a complicated subject and breaks it down into plain English, allowing for concepts, definitions, and so much more to be absorbed and understood. It offers a detailed understanding of what is crucial in Business Continuity Management, and the practical steps and stories help the reader implement each phase of planning including: Project Management, Gap Analysis, Risk Evaluation Business Impact Analysis, Strategic Planning, Emergency Response and

Operations, Awareness and Training, Maintaining and Exercising Plans, Public Relations and Crisis Coordination, and more.

Unlike other books where you are offered only a checklist, this book teaches though stories, practical applications, and yes, bullet pointed checklists, too.

Mastering Your Work Life Balance

Work Life Balance is a challenge for many people. It involves learning and implementing new skills, such as goal setting, concentration, releasing procrastination, releasing unwanted stress, better time management, and finding your purpose in life.

You may feel that work life balance can only happen in the future when everything is settled, such as your career is perfect, your relationship is perfect, or you are perfect. Not so. With the step-by-step guidelines and exercises presented in this book, you can experience change this month.

Work life balance applies not only to those working in formal jobs. You could be a parent who's balancing the needs of your children with your own. You could be a grandparent who wants to "be there" for your children and grandchildren, but you want to have time to finally do all the things retirement is supposed to allow.

Imagine a world where you have time for your career, family, friends, health, happiness, hobbies, travel, and more. You're setting forward looking goals that excite and encourage you in all areas of your life.

Start your new life of Mastering Your Work Life Balance by reading this book today!

Mastering Your Introduction to Cyber Security

Cyber-attacks have increased exponentially, making this book essential in areas such as Business Management, Business Continuity and Disaster Recovery, Risk Management, Compliance, and IT.

Dr. Michael C. Redmond, PhD takes a complicated subject and breaks it down into plain English, allowing you to understand and absorb the information easily. Unlike other books where you think you've learned the information provided, this book's chapter tests, along with the answer key at the end, ensure your understanding is complete.

PECB University

Aspirations for the establishment of PECB University extend beyond years of devoted commitment and relentless efforts to design and develop a unique set of arrangements necessary to meet the challenges of the modern society. The idea generated from Mr. Eric Lachapelle and Mr. Faton Aliu, founders of PECB Inc., who, accounting for the success of PECB as a global training provider, sought to identify new opportunities for expansion in the market of educational services. The positive feedback and the constant return of certified professionals for additional trainings landed greater support to the view that new options could be explored and exploited to provide additional appealing opportunities for further academic advancements. Accounting for the already established reputation as a provider of professional trainings, and being able to associate elements of comparability between the provided trainings and courses of higher education around the content, extent, and quality, the idea to offer encompassing programs that lead to graduate certificates and degrees appeared even more possible.

The initial efforts unfolded with an overview of the existent higher education offerings so to familiarize with common practices but at the same time to identify innovative possibilities that would attract the interest of modern learners. Hence the determination to offer degrees in rather new specializations and in untraditional formats that allow for extending knowledge to farther regions regardless of physical boundaries. The efforts progressed with the design of graduate and degree programs which was done in close collaboration with field experts, faculty and staff to achieve a combination of offerings that would best satisfy the interests of diverse candidates. The development of such program offerings emerged in light of the evolvement that higher education has experienced in the past decade while striving to adjust to rapidly changing needs of society, economy, and workforce. As a result of three years of considerable commitment, PECB University, has achieved a competent faculty body and a strong organizational structure to support its operations, and is finally ready to welcome its first generation of graduate students.

Built upon a foundation that has student experience at the center of attention, the University is bound to regard highly the aspirations of each student. We are confident that our students will learn to embrace challenging situations and thus become prepared to take essential responsibilities in managing challenges and transforming them into favorable opportunities. The University takes pride in offering learning opportunities that exploit technological advancements to the benefit of students so that they are not limited of opportunities to excel in corresponding prospects. The combination of success factors including technology for sharing across space and time, specialized programs, and qualified faculty will be a strong starting point for many years of success ahead.

PECB University is an independent institution of higher education focused on business education, which is inspired by the tenets of professionalism of its parent company, PECB Inc. – a world-class certification body for persons on international standards. Based on this premise, PECB University seeks to build upon this established expertise, and provide future-proof academic specializations, aimed at using coherent and updated curriculum to add value to the professional development of its students, so that students in turn, will have the skills and knowledge to make an impact on their workplace, innovate and become pioneers of change.

PECB University's mission is to provide top quality graduate level education, unique professional development opportunities and comprehensive learning management services that inspire continuous improvement, bridge the gap between academia and the labor market, and provide knowledge that benefit individuals, change organizations, and impact the society.

PECB

PECB is a certification body that provides education, certification, and certificate programs for individuals on a wide range of disciplines. Through PECB's presence in more than 150 countries, the aim is to help professionals demonstrate their competence in various areas of expertise by providing valuable evaluation, certification, and certificate programs against internationally recognized standards.

The key objectives are:

- Establishing the minimum requirements necessary to certify professionals and to grant designations
- Reviewing and verifying the qualifications of individuals to ensure they are eligible for certification

- Maintaining and continually improving the evaluation process for certifying individuals
- Certifying qualified individuals, granting designations and maintaining respective directories
- Establishing requirements for the periodic renewal of certifications and ensuring that the certified individuals are complying with those requirements
- Ascertaining that PECB professionals meet ethical standards in their professional practice
- Representing our stakeholders in matters of common interest
- Promoting the benefits of certification and certificate programs to professionals, businesses, governments, and the public

PECB's mission is to provide clients with comprehensive examination, certification, and certificate program services that inspire trust and benefit the society as a whole.

PECB continuously publishes topmost innovative training courses through its best experts in the field for the provision of education, certification, and certificate program services. PECB's expertise is in multiple fields, with a special emphasis in Information Security and Resilience, Cybersecurity, and Continuity, Resilience, and Recovery, Governance, Risk, and Compliance, Privacy and Data Protection, as well as in Quality and Management, Health and Safety, and Sustainability. .

▶ Accreditations

The value of PECB certifications is validated by the accreditation from the International Accreditation Service (IAS-PCB-111), the United Kingdom Accreditation Service (UKAS-No. 21923), and the Korean Accreditation Board (KAB-PC-08) under ISO/IEC 17024 – General requirements for bodies operating certification of persons. The value of PECB certificate programs is validated by the accreditation from the ANSI National Accreditation Board (ANAB-Accreditation ID 1003) under ANSI/ASTM E2659-18, Standard Practice for Certificate Programs.

Furthermore, PECB is an associate member of The Independent Association of Accredited Registrars (IAAR), a full member of the International Personnel Certification Association (IPC), a signatory member of IPC MLA, and a member of Club EBIOS, CPD Certification Service, CLUSIF, Credential Engine, and ITCC. In addition, PECB is an approved Licensed Partner Publisher (LPP) from the Cybersecurity Maturity Model Certification Accreditation Body (CMMC-AB) for the Cybersecurity Maturity Model Certification standard (CMMC), is approved by Club EBIOS to offer the EBIOS Risk Manager Skills certification, and is approved by CNIL (Commission Nationale de l'Informatique et des Libertés) to offer DPO certification.

▶ The Value of PECB Certification

PECB credentials are internationally recognized and endorsed by many accreditation bodies, so professionals who pursue them will benefit from our recognition in domestic and international markets.

High-quality products and services

PECB provides clients with high-quality products and services that match their needs and demands. All products are carefully prepared by a team of experts and professionals based on the best practices and methodologies.

Compliance with standards

The PECB certifications and certificate programs are a demonstration of compliance with ISO/IEC 17024 and ASTM E2659. They ensure that the standard requirements have been fulfilled and validated with adequate consistency, professionalism, and impartiality.